Nick Cave's Bar

by Aug Stone

First printing: 2020

ISBN 978-1-0879-2907-1

www.augstone.com

Cover design by Christine Navin

Lyrics from 'Straight To You', 'From Her To Eternity', 'Red Right Hand', 'I Let Love In', 'Nobody's Baby Now', 'Hallelujah', and 'Papa Won't Leave You, Henry' by Nick Cave & The Bad Seeds are reprinted by kind permission from the author

Lyrics from 'Strasbourg' by Julian Cope are reprinted by kind permission from the author

Lyrics from 'The Luckiest Guy on the Lower East Side' by The Magnetic Fields are reprinted by kind permission from the author

Excerpts from Vladimir Nabokov's *Transparent Things* and *The Eye* are reprinted with kind permission from Penguin Random House *for Andy*

Introduction – 'The Days Of Rainbows'

In June 1999, my best friend and I flew to Germany to find the bar I'd heard Nick Cave owned in Berlin. In our heads we'd get off the plane, ask 'which way to Nick Cave's bar?', and then spend the rest of our time living it up amidst the wild world of its confines. Instead what followed were nine days of confusion, thwarted plans, and perpetual drunken misery. Nevertheless, I look back on it all with great fondness. 2019 marked the 20th anniversary of our trip. To this day, I'm not sure Nick Cave ever owned a bar in Berlin.

I – 'I Wanna Tell Ya About A Girl'

It all started with a woman named Kate. No, not that one. Or that one. See, women named Kate have always had a big effect on my life – the red-haired high school crush who one night asked me to come out with her and her friends and oh how I couldn't believe it when the words materializing from my mouth somehow declined the offer, making for much regret, or my teenage torch who I never got the chance to tell how I truly felt, causing years of the same. And then there's my partner-in-Pop over in London, with whom I've had many a musical adventure. Expand this to Katherine, Kathryn, and Catherine, and the effects go on and on. Now that I think about it, that first woman I mentioned was Katie. An 'i' in there, a '1' if you will, for our paths only ever intersected on that single occasion. But, oh, what an impact her words were to have on my life.

I met Katie at a hostel in Barcelona where she was working. She was friends with a guy named Paul with whom I had spent the day playing chess. I think they may have dated when they lived in Berlin. Their story was never entirely clear, but they had recently moved to Spain, if not together, then at the same time, and seemed to get along fine. Paul was from Arizona, Katie Australia. I lost most of the chess matches, which is no real surprise. My approach to the game was much like my approach to living at that time – adopt no real strategy and just see what happens. At some point, though, you've got to have a plan, or else you'll be down to your solitary king, scrambling for your life as the ravens and rooks take wing. You'll see. That evening, after play had exhausted and the pieces were packed away, we all went to the beach with a bottle of red. Strolling through a public square, I turned to Katie and asked, 'Do you like Nick Cave?'

'Man, I'm Australian. I love Nick Cave. He owns a bar in Berlin, you know. I always meant to go when I lived there.'

But this all really starts with a girl named Terri. One of those girls everyone falls in love with. And I'd been for two years at that point. Shortly after I first met her, I hesitated one night when I should have kissed her and she quickly became one of my best friends. Tough thing being in love with one of your best friends. Even tougher to have a close friend be in love with you. But I valued our friendship enormously. For in those dark times of your late teens and early twenties, when you're just trying to exist and find out who you are, and the world doesn't seem to much care about either, often appearing to insist on the former while stripping you of the latter, I felt that Terri actually did care. If ever I was sad, which I often was, Terri would take me out on her front porch and we'd sit and smoke cigarettes and talk. I have a feeling this kind of stuff is normal for most people. But for me, intensely shy by nature, who lives so much in his own head and almost entirely so in those days, I found this both wonderful and scary. And most of all rare.

I say 'intensely shy by nature', but that's only part of it. I've delved deep into Chinese metaphysics the past five years and this is one of the characteristics of the Fire Dragon, the year I was born. But the day I was born was the day of the Fire Horse, which being doubly Yang Fire, is the most extroverted of all the animals in the Zodiac. It is the pull between these two energies that symbolizes what I am. A metaphysics teacher summed it up best with 'You have a great desire to be seen, and also a terrible fear of it'. That could be why I write – to be out there but from a safe middle distance. This is all relevant to what's coming, trust me. Also of note on the Chinese Astrology tip is that all this Fire, and a constant seeking to cool it down with, what else, Water, may very well be why I drank so much. I have noticed that like me, the star charts of my friends with Horse and Dragon in their make-ups all seem to be able to drink astronomical amounts of alcohol. My future traveling companion also has Dragon and Horse in his chart. You'll meet him soon.

Back to Terri. After graduating Boston University in 1998, we decided to backpack around Europe together. She was going for three months or so and I would join her for the first leg of her journey, a month and a half from Amsterdam to Rome, counter-clockwise. From the get-go, we had wildly different ideas of what we wanted from the trip and she must've thought I was joking when

I told her I planned on being drunk the whole time, keen to see what European nightlife had to offer. The final straw came only a week into it, when I left Notre-Dame cathedral after only five minutes to go to the Paris Rough Trade record shop. I have no regrets about this. I fondly recall holding The Springfields' 'Wonder' 7" single, Sarah Records SARAH40, in my hands and weighing up the chances of the vinyl not breaking in my rucksack. Sarah is another huge name in my life, but that's a whole other story, probably many more. Ultimately I put the record back on the shelf, the risk being too great, but I would think of this often until I finally found the single again at the Notting Hill Music Exchange in London some years later. Rough Trade Paris isn't there anymore and I can find little information about it on the internet. I'm so glad I went. Ascending up that tiny back staircase, to the angelic sounds of the records above. Notre-Dame, I have always reasoned, will be there forever should I ever feel I need more time in it. In twenty years I haven't. Though I was a little shaken while working on an early draft of this story, when the news came that the cathedral had caught fire. So much for assumptions...

I'll freely admit I'm not the easiest travelling companion. It often takes me days to adjust to jetlag, and staying true to my m.o. of being 'all about the nightlife', sleeping all day in Amsterdam and Brussels seemed simply a necessary prerequisite. Arising at 4 PM local Belgian time, I felt refreshed and ready. In my youthful idiocy I was genuinely surprised to find that Terri, who had spent the day sightseeing alone, was not pleased with my behavior, and her admonishment that 'you'll never get to sleep at night if you sleep all day' I felt missed the point. Remember my awesome m.o.?

Sensing something was 'off', I decided not to head to the nearest bar and instead opted to look for something cultural to do in these environs. With my childhood love for Asterix and Tintin springing back to life from being around so much *bande dessinee*, I suggested we visit the Comics Art Museum, full of the most excellent exhibits. Years later, I would recall this excursion when, doubting my own credentials, I nonetheless became the first Comics Editor for The Quietus. I have little knowledge of superheroes, but, in those three years, I did hip the world to some very cool European artists.

Buying frites at a kebob shop later that night, the man behind the counter greeted our American accents with 'America! Miami Vice!' It was 1998 and that this was the impression our country gave off pleased me to no end. *This* memory burst its way back to me when I created the character of Don Johnson, a blacklisted C.I.A. agent who joins forces with 18th Century Albanian Poetry Professor Donald Fox, for *The Oxford Dons*, the wonderfully absurd and ridiculous short film and radio play I would write with Jamie Manners in 2009 and 2010. An experience so rewarding and enjoyable that, little did I know at the time, would pave the way for what I'm doing now with Young Southpaw. Plenty of little meaningful moments like these would keep appearing - I find in life they always do - as we'll soon see from that one sentence spoken to me in Barcelona a week later.

I'd be remiss not to recount the fact that this was my first ever visit to Paris. The City Of Light, The City Of Love.

And oh how true I found these appellations to be, made all the more poignant by being there without them. For it was plain to see how wonderful it would be to wander those timeless streets together with your heart's desire. A keen, sharp sadness I have felt every time I've been there, always alone, always aware. And being so near, in physical space at least, to my own impossible wish, who by then was drifting even further away. But lest I miss out on any details of drunken adventures to come, I should note we spent a pre-Paris night in Strasbourg on the way. I suggested this stopover simply because I've always liked Julian Cope's song of the same name from the *World Shut Your Mouth* album - 'If I were France and you were Germany, what an alliance that would be'. To my utter surprise, my traveling companion agreed to go. We hopped off in Luxembourg en route to while away the afternoon and I found myself quite taken with the valley in the middle of the city. Six years later, when I moved to London, my favourite band bore the same name as this country and capital. The perfect cross between Suede and Pulp, I followed them fanatically and would eventually work with each member in some musical capacity, most notably with singer David Shah as The Soft Close-Ups.

Our friend Sia was spending a semester abroad in 'gay Pairee' and had offered us a place to crash. It is important to note here that when I was getting ready for this trip, everything I needed for five weeks in one 40-pound backpack, I made a conscious decision not to bring any music with me. Figuring out what albums to have on my person, at the ready, has always been an excruciating decision for me – you never know what you'll want to listen to at any given time. So to deal with this problem I used to bring as much as I possibly could, family vacations weighed down by whole dufflebags full of cassettes. After I left such a sack in a New Orleans hotel room when I was twelve, my father having to race back for it and narrowly missing our plane home, my parents limited the amount of tapes I could take to forty. Paring them down to even that number was almost impossible. Six months earlier, in March of 1998, I had bought my 1000th cd – the Jesus & Mary Chain's *Honey's Dead*, a very important album for me that I'd had on cassette since

1992 – and I threw a party to celebrate. One of my best friends, and an equally-as-obsessed music buyer, Brian, then heavily getting into old jazz, bought me my 1001st, *Back To Back: Duke Ellington & Johnny Hodges Play The Blues*, and gave it to me at the party. The day of the event, taking place in Allston, Massachusetts, I drove the two-and-a-half hours down to Connecticut to pick up two other very good friends and fellow music fanatics, Jon & Jim, and bring them back up for the festivities. After all the countless hours we logged traveling to record shop after record shop and just talking about music, it seemed only right that they should be there with me. Jon making the trip up from Baltimore especially for this and Jim, who in high school I once loaned seventy-five tapes to it in a single go, now owns close to 16,000 records himself. The very next day the three of us went record shopping in Harvard Square and I bought twelve more cds, bringing my total up to 1013. I still have the receipt from this momentous occasion. The two cds that stand out are Pharoah Sanders' *Karma* and Nick Cave & The Bad Seeds' *From Her To Eternity*.

Unbeknownst to me at the time, my friends Andy and Tim, well aware of my cd buying habits, were making a concerted effort to get me into Nick Cave. I only had *The Boatman's Call* before I met them and they knew that, with a little talking-up on their part, I'd buy the rest of the albums they wanted to hear. By the time I left for this European trip six months later, I owned pretty much all of Nick Cave's releases.

And on September 7th, a few days before I flew to Amsterdam, I saw him live for the first time on the Greatest Hits tour at The Roxy in Boston. It was an excellent show. I was somewhat nervous being a newbie surrounded by all these hardcore fans. A woman showing up in a wedding dress, looking fantastic, and one of the bouncers asking her if she was going to marry Nick Cave. I was flying out from New York and drove back to my hometown in Connecticut a few days later, buying the *Greatest Hits* cd, along with Saint Etienne's *Good Humor* album, both with bonus discs, at Secret Sounds in Bridgeport, CT. These I would save until I got back from my trip, and it rekindled an intense love for Saint Etienne.

Catching them live that December 13th at The Paradise began a series of events that would later see me move to London to record with their producer Ian Catt, fall in love all over again with that city, live there for the better part of ten years, and interview the band three times.

I also stopped at Barnes & Noble after Secret Sounds, excited they had Ian Johnston's *Bad Seed: The Biography Of Nick Cave* in stock, and snatched that right up for the trip. I brought five books with me, though now I only recall *Bad Seed* and Martin Amis' *Other People*. Once in Europe I would also purchase Kingsley Amis' *Lucky Jim* (a comedy to cheer me up, procured in Zurich, shortly after Terri and I parted ways), Martin Amis' *Night Train*, and Jean-Paul Sartre's *Nausea* to deal with my existential crisis from the fall-out.

Carrying around these books, but no music, was an experiment. One with harrowing results. I had thought, long and hard, about bringing my Walkman - this was 1998 after all - and making just five mixtapes of the essentials. But no, I decided I would let my ears soak up all the local culture of wherever we were, keep myself open to new sounds, the world of possibilities traveling down the ether and headed straight for your heart. But then you're on a train for a silent six hours, or, as a lifelong insomniac, trying to get to sleep at night, and sad sad sad at how everything's turned out. To just have those songs with you would mean everything. And they weren't. Because you decided to 'experiment'. Music, my salvation over the years, would have indeed rescued me many a time on that trip.

When we got to Sia's place in Paris she had a boombox and a handful of tapes. Listening to The Pixies' *Doolittle* and *Bagsy Me* by The Wannadies refreshed my very soul. I would return to Paris a little over a week later, on my own this time, all conversation with my traveling companion and any enjoyment of spending time together having run its course. I was desperate for company and Sia has always been a great friend. When she was at class, those cassettes filled a very real hole in my being. But before that...

Terri and I left Paris after a few days, heading to Bordeaux with the intention to drink wine. I don't recall us speaking much after Notre-Dame except her being really annoyed that it 'sounded like a marching band' in Sia's dorm, keeping her awake all night, and me wishing there was something I could do about it. Of note, however, is that on our first day in Paris, we headed up to Sacré-Couer with its magnificent view of the city. And when she asked me 'Where to next?', I led us down the back, away from all that. Oh how embarrassed I was when Terri said with a smile 'You know, everything is the other way'. This incident seems to sum up something essential about my character, especially back then, when I was painfully unaware of it. I'd have everything in front of me and then turn 180 degrees because I thought there must be more elsewhere too. Enchantments beyond the visible, like so much going on in my mind. So I'd never move towards an objective, except the vague goal of wandering without ever arriving. Inherent in this is a perpetual dissatisfaction. Situations made impossible by the fear that when you get there, it might not be what you want at all, or even close to what you have in your head.

Back to Chinese astrology, this is very much a Dragon characteristic. The Dragon has been described to me as 'a wide open door', but instead of going thru it, the immature Dragon simply fantasizes about all that might be beyond all the other infinite yet invisible doors.

By Bordeaux Terri and I were barely speaking and once aboard the long train to Madrid two days later, all conversation had ceased. I quite liked Madrid, it reminded me of New York City in a way. I was on my own now and, per usual, looking to distract myself from all these feelings I could barely contain. I popped into a book store, bought Martin Amis' newly published *Night Train* from their small English-language section, and sat reading that dark, dark novella in the blessed air-conditioning. Upon leaving, only minutes back out into this sultry September, returning to a cool dark room seemed just the thing when a cinema marquee announced *Night Watch* was showing. The Ewan McGregor morgue murder movie, not the overshadowing Russian supernatural thriller which anyways hadn't yet been released.

They say the Universe reflects back what's going on inside yourself and this was grim subject matter indeed staring at me from page and screen. Only now do I notice the two Night's of that day in Madrid. But make no mistake, this was Night.

Perhaps it's a condition of Youth, some youths anyway, that we're not conscious enough to see what's really going on. We only sense something very wrong and we immediately try to numb out even those first sensations of pain with whatever's at hand – drink, drugs, sex, food, record shopping, etc. – anything not to feel it, not to hear its message. And despite darkness now setting in from without, to reinforce what my internal emissaries had been shouting all along, I remained oblivious to any of this. I was mistaking Night to be a time to keep dreaming. To keep running possibilities through my head where they couldn't go as wrong as in real life. But none of this seemed to be present at the time in my surface consciousness that just wanted to get drunk and entertain. Despite Terri and my now rapidly deteriorating friendship showing me how untenable the whole situation was, I couldn't see any of this. As Mr. Cave sings in 'Papa Won't Leave You, Henry' – my grandfather's name by the way, whose own father died when he was just five years old - 'The night is dark and the night is deep and its jaws are open wide'. Night, indeed.

Back in Allston, my friend Ry – an Insane Clown Posse fan from the very beginning - would dub the years around this time 'The Dark Carnival'. It most certainly was. But back outside this cinema in Madrid, it was only late afternoon and I couldn't go wrong with this plan to see a film, relax in a cool dim room, and eat some popcorn. Although I had taken Spanish in high school, upon arriving in Spain the only words I could remember were 'queso' and 'helado', and so hopping off the train at 1 AM I found an open diner and promptly ordered a cheese sandwich and chocolate ice cream after seven hungry hours on a wordless train. But this was an English-language movie, I would be fine while the Spanish speakers read the subtitles. Once the film began however, it was, of course, dubbed.

Unenamored with Madrid, Terri wanted to move on, and I, hoping this radio silence was just a phase, agreed. We pressed on to Barcelona. Another long train journey with no communication. We checked into a hostel and it was there we met Katie and Paul. I spent a couple days smoking strong French cigarettes and playing chess with the latter. One afternoon out exploring the city solo, as I walked along the beach with the Mediterranean looking so beautiful, so inviting, I stripped down to my boxer shorts and ran straight in. It seems to me one of the few spontaneous things I ever did in my youth, and, my goodness, was it wonderful.

One evening Katie invited us down to the shore with Paul and some others to drink red wine. Terri seemed in a much better mood now. I didn't know it at the time, but she had met a fella and would end up spending a couple months with him. On the beach, as we passed the bottle around, Paul told us how, when he was young, his dad had been working away from home for a very long time. When he returned, he had a giant beard and Paul thought it was Santa Claus come early. Funny the things you remember. Shortly after the beach, towards 11 at night, we were in a small crowded public square when it happened.

Me: Katie, do you like Nick Cave?

Katie: Man, I'm Australian. I love Nick Cave. He owns a bar in Berlin, you know. I always meant to go when I lived there.

And this was all I needed to hear. I split the next day when Terri told me she had no interest in seeing Switzerland. I remember being so sad for a moment and then my fiery Aries tendencies carrying me out that hostel door as quick as they could to the bus station, an intoxicating sense of freedom numbing all the pain I couldn't bring myself to face. I took a long bus ride through a dark, dark night reading *Bad Seed*, arriving in Zurich late the next morning. I fell in love with that city. Visiting James Joyce's grave, in that small cemetery on top of the hill with its stunning view of the mountains, was the most peaceful I have ever felt in my life. Needing some comic relief, I bought Kingsley Amis' *Lucky Jim* in a small book shop in the center of town. The Amises were certainly with me through some bleak, lonely moments on that trip. Desperate for some real-life company, I went back to Paris a few days later, arriving early and shivering through the morning in a cold, misty park until I felt it was a reasonable time to phone Sia. Spending those few days with friends, people I could talk and laugh with, felt as good as getting to listen to music again. Terri and I had made plans to meet in Florence a week later. When I got to the appointed hostel, there was the message 'I'm in Rome'. Nothing more than that. As my return ticket to the States had me departing from that eternal city two weeks later, I decided to head there and get a flight back early. I made a couple half-hearted attempts to phone a hostel or two to see if Ter was there, but really I just wanted to get home. And this was quite a strong urge because my itinerary included some time in London, my favourite city in the world, before flying back to New York. But I changed things up to only spend one day in The Big Smoke, to, of course, get some serious record shopping done.

It is significant to point out that behind where the Virgin Records used to sit on Oxford Street back then lies Hanway Street, home to The Troy Club and On The Beat Records, the first atop the latter. And on that day in October 1998 in the record shop underneath, I found the three-track Nick Cave & The Bad Seeds acoustic sessions bonus disc that came with *Tender Prey*. Only recently has The Troy Club borne the 'TROY 22' sign, but when I first moved to London in 2003 it was still unmarked, up a dark stairway where on any given night eighty or so boisterous drinkers would be crowded into a room with a capacity of only twenty-five. A glorious afterhours find, first discovered while I was out scouting Britpop landmarks my first week after settling in. Falling in with three Croatian punk rock girls at The Good Mixer, as one of their boyfriends ushered us into a cab at chucking out time, he whispered to me 'I don't know if this place still exists, but I don't want them to be disappointed'. That was seventeen years ago, long may it thrive. Since then I have been convinced that this special spot – record store below, speakeasy on top, where you could always feel the magic in the air, and that initially brought me that bonus disc just when I needed it – is situated along one of Bill Drummond's interstellar ley lines.

I flew home, a mess. In one of the magazines I bought for the flight there was a short interview with Nick Cave in which he revealed he was reading Evelyn Waugh's *A Handful Of Dust*. I made a note to get this novel as soon as I could. I loved Waugh and still do. The thing I value most from my university education was being introduced to him, via *Vile Bodies*. Once the plane touched down, I stayed at my parents for a week in Connecticut. My mother observing that I looked stunned and later commenting on how I would just sit in their living room listening to Cave's 'Straight To You' on repeat. Man, I love that song. It has always resonated with me. 'Gone are the days of rainbows, and gone are the nights of swinging from the stars'. Indeed.

Soon I returned to Allston, MA. It was of vital importance to tell Andy, my friend who had maneuvered my Nick Cave fandom, that the man himself owned a bar in Berlin. This was 1998. I had not been on the internet more than a handful of times at that point in my life. I gave Andy the news and without doing any further research, we decided to go.

II – 'Catastrophic Plan'

Back in the States, I found myself in the post-collegiate world, the one where you're supposed to figure out how to become an adult while also keeping to your nightly drinking schedule. A routine that in Boston began around 11 PM. With a temp job looming in the morning, every evening the call would come, on a landline back then, with tones that always expressed our having hit upon a genius new idea - 'Silhouette? Then The Model?' And we would meet at The Swill, as our first port of call was affectionately known, with its cheap pitchers of watery beer, free popcorn, and darts, stay until its closing time of 1 AM, then proceed to make our way up the street to the latter, where we'd finish out the last hour of the city's official bar times. After two hours of bargain bullpen drinking, all sense of budgeting would be thrown out the window as we hit The Model, sampling any concoction that struck our fancy. My cauldronesque stomach has never had a problem mixing various boozes and back then on any given night a Midori Sour, Tequila Sunrise, 7 & 7, the sweet Chambord of a Grape Crush, Malibu &

Coke, Old Fashioned, Long Island Iced Tea, Singapore Sling, Alabama Slammer, Gin & Tonic, and ever-fun Holy Grail of the Evening, Boilermaker, might find their way in. Though I usually would stick to vodka-based beverages, my Russian blood allowing me to imbibe a vast array until the korovas come home. Amongst all this, bottles of beer always found their way into your hands. Along with free smokes. The cigarette companies had just begun their campaigns of giving you packs gratis in exchange for your address. Your physical one that is, I wouldn't have checked my old college email address for months at this point and was still a ways away from my friend Rick signing me up for a Hotmail account. When I finally quit smoking – February 11th, 2000 – I was sucking down two-and-a-half packs a day, simply because the supply was there. Crazy to think about now.

Once back out The Model's doors, usually for us around 2:20 AM, if you were to head down Brighton Ave. towards the intersection with Harvard Ave., keeping The Silhouette to your right, as you would if you were going back to Andy's place on Linden Street, you would pass what was known as 'The Allston Mall'. A rickety wooden structure atop a row of restaurants, on the left-hand side of the street, with two dark staircases on either end leading in and out. Standing at the bottom of one of these, looking up into that shadowy interior and wondering if there was actually anything up there, you'd be filled with a keen desire to, for the first time in your life, have fire code information at the ready. But on that upper floor lay magic. Mars Records seemed to appear there out of nowhere one day, beginning life as just one small room. One that was, however, filled with an incredible amount of albums I'd been looking for for ages. There I found many a Teardrop Explodes 7" and those first couple James singles, Jim1 and Jim2, artefacts I'd never dared hope to actually behold, let alone be able to so readily purchase. Across from Mars was Garage Video. An actual video shop with such a large and strange assortment, any twenty-one-year-old indie-rocker would lose their pretense of cool within seconds of perusing the tapes on offer. I recall the VHS of the French film *Sex Shop* for which Serge Gainsbourg composed the lovely, as haunting as it is exquisite, title track. Flooding through me was a mixture of excitement at finding such a rarity and embarrassment at the thought of someone seeing me carrying such a video whose title might suggest other things besides its film score. As I took it in my hands, these feelings were immediately squashed when Garage owner Will warned me that this version was 'dubbed'. I wouldn't have minded but the combination of sorrow and annoyance in his voice as he relayed this information made me think I might be betraying something sacred were I to ever rent this video, despite him having it for such a purpose on the shelves of his shop. To this day, I have never watched the movie, nor seen a copy since. Despite the ramshackle nature of these surroundings, I'm still grateful to Will and the owners of Mars for providing me access to such culture right on my doorstep, The Allston Mall having been just around the corner from my first ever apartment. These places, along with Diskovery underneath, street level on Brighton Ave., gave us access to the books, records, and films that so much go into the shaping of young lives.

At some point during 1998 Andy rented *Nick Cave & The Bad Seeds: The Videos* from Garage, and as far as I know has still not returned it. Its overdueness became somewhat of a joke after three weeks. But the humor soon turned to a mixture of discomfort and embarrassment. As the months dragged on, there was no way he could give it back now, couldn't even set foot in the shop to rent more of the enticing films we wanted to see - it had been far too long. And besides, its viewing had become part of our nightly ritual. We'd return from The Model, careful not to wake Andy's two roommates, pop in the tape, and settle into his dark front room. It seems absurd to think of it now, that at 2:30 in the morning we'd watch all 98 minutes of the video, and then, always being one to prefer my own bed to a less comfortable couch, I'd walk the twenty minutes home to fall asleep around 4:30. But such a sequence surely happened, and regularly. After a while, in a strange drunken sense of order that we were unable to impose on the other 23 hours of the day, we would pick the videos we wanted to see most and only watch these highlights before calling it a night. There'd always be talk of 'crying', and although this was a joke, there were certainly nights where we'd fall silent in the shadows of the living room, each ruminating on the seemingly all-enveloping despair of our current states of being. Lovelives and lackthereof especially, with which Nick Cave's songs resonate so well.

Andy and I were becoming best friends. My best friend at the time was Perry, who was Andy's best friend from high school. Making Andy and I somewhat best-friends-in-law. Perry had a steady job and a girlfriend that year after college and the two of them were planning on moving to the West Coast. With such a shake-up looming, Andy and I began to spend more and more time together. Our mutual ability to consume far more alcohol than your average drinker quickly facilitated slipping into a deeper friendship. But really what I think bonded us, and of course this ties into the drinking, was our shared sense that sabotage could be just as satisfying as success. A girl named Lisa, who you'll meet in a minute, once said that I was always happy because I was always smiling. Andy quickly set her straight by revealing that 'Aug isn't happy. Aug's always smiling because he's thinking of the most deviant thing he could possibly be doing.' And when I heard this, I realized that somebody finally got it, had in fact picked up on this – I fully admit unhealthy – vibe without me ever having to explain. Months later, during one of our first days in Berlin, Andy said to me 'I just like fucking people over. It doesn't matter who it is, myself included.' We were very much in the same boat, floating atop tidal waves of intoxicants, both prepared to dive but neither to take the oars and row to safety.

Our friendship really solidified during what became known as 'The Twelve Nights'. In late January of 1999, our friends Sia, Jess, and Kelly had all returned from semesters abroad and threw a party in their new apartment. There was so much alcohol left over, Andy and I volunteered to come back and help drink it every night until it was gone. We declared this would take a further eleven visits and on the final evening, in accordance with the occasion, we would perform a rendition of Shakespeare's 'Twelfth Night'. Our estimate was wildly inaccurate as the surplus bottles and keg were finished off the following evening, but we kept our word and brought our own provisions for the remaining ten sessions. One of these evenings saw the invention of 'The Junkyard'. Named after The Birthday Party song and album, its ingredients are of the moment - one simply pours what is left in the various bottles of Night's end into a glass and imbibes. It is usually unpleasant, but it serves its purpose. Two years later, our friend Megan threw a party ending with another such overflow situation. Andy and I were called in on the Monday to 'clean up'. We finished the job remarkably quickly, though of course calling such an event 'The One Night' would be problematic. However, we soon became known as The ODDs – Official Designated Drinkers - and when a post-party apartment was facing similar circumstances, who you gonna call? Well, us, if you don't mind that we never actually perform 'Twelfth Night'.

I had known Lisa for two years at this point and, while we weren't close friends, in December she was looking for some new music, and I made her a mix tape. She liked it so much that at The Twelve Nights, I was figuring out what songs would be on the next one. Amidst all the general talk of Nick Cave, Andy and I spent an inordinate amount of time debating the perfect Bad Seeds song to go on this mix. In a box in my closet I still have most of my handwritten notes for the mix tapes I made girls between 1994-2002. Consulting these, which bear early track orders and possible contenders, it seems I eventually narrowed our choices down to 'Lime Tree Arbour' and 'The Ship Song'. And checking the final cut, the former won out. This amazes me to think about now, for though I love both songs dearly, and have always been very fond of 'Lime Tree Arbour', it is 'The Ship Song' that reminds me of that time in my life, and over the years the one that has remained in my Top Ten Nick Cave Songs. The others being – at this time of this writing, June 2019 - 'Straight To You', 'Deanna', 'Papa Won't Leave You, Henry', 'Good Good Day', 'New Morning', 'Sad Waters', 'Black Hair', 'Tupelo', and 'Rings Of Saturn'. With 'Rock Of Gibraltar' a close eleventh.

The mix tape was not, at first, a romantic gesture. I simply love introducing people to awesome music. And I was touched that Lisa appreciated the first batch enough to ask me for a second one. It was here that, per usual, my musical excitement obliterated any common sense and I was to learn, thru Andy, that Nick Cave & Anita Lane's version of 'Je T'Aime...Moi Non Plus' made Lisa feel uncomfortable. To my ears it's the gorgeousness of the music that draws you in. To others, it's Anita Lane making sex sounds that strikes them most about the song. I didn't mean anything by this, I had also put it on a mix for my family's vacation in Florida the previous summer. I simply adored the melody. I can be that oblivious at times.

I ended up making Lisa half a dozen mixes in the space of one year. Three through six did not go as I intended. But while we're still on mix number two, I should tell you about Mod Night and its role in furthering the infatuation. Around the corner from the Allston Mall if you set out in the direction of The Model and take your first right lies The Common Ground, which on Wednesday evenings was host to 'What A Way To Go-Go', though referred to by all as 'Mod Night'. DJ Vin spun mostly English records, from the 60s to the ragged ends of Britpop that we were facing at the time. The Kinks, The Stone Roses, Blur, Suede, Erasure, New Order. It was my idea of heaven. Afterwards we all used to go back to Lisa's house and one night I ended up accidentally passing out in her bed. And then did so again the following week. And the next. Again, the first couple times were completely innocent. On one of those mornings I woke up not knowing where I was, so I lightly kicked the blanket next to me. She popped her head out and we both started laughing. This was fun, staying up most of the night, talking and getting to know each other better. The mix tapes continued and eventually we kissed. She was an amazing kisser. I fell for her in a big way, but it was not to be. Thankfully we stayed friends and I used to let her drive my car sometimes. When I got my Nissan Maxima - chosen simply for its dark shade of my favourite green and Bose stereo system – Lisa drove us up to Newbury Street to go record shopping. Having recently heard 'C'est La Vie', I was standing at the Imports section with the B*Witched cd in my hand, when she came up and told me that if I bought said compact disc she would 'never speak to me again'. I put it back on the shelf. The last time I saw Lisa was at a bar in NYC a year or so later, and we were discussing the latest, sixth and last, mix I had made and posted to her in Ohio. With its 'cause I've got wheels and you wanna go for a ride', I told her The Magnetic Fields' 'Luckiest Guy On The Lower East Side' reminded me of her. She smiled and said 'I know it does'.

Sometime in the winter of 1999, it was pointed out that Andy and I were indeed 'best friends'. I remember both of us shifting uncomfortably in our seats on perpendicular couches as this was revealed, Andy even calling attention to the fact that 'this has never been said out loud before'. It was true of course, but oh the risk if the other didn't feel the same way. I'd been burned by this in the past. The summer after fourth grade, a camp counselor asked my best friend Brian, the one who later bought me my 1001st cd, if we were best friends. He replied, 'I'm his best friend, but my best friend is Nate.' I can laugh about it now but at the time it was...probably even funnier.

Shortly after this revelation, Andy's parents decided to give him a gift. Money he could use to do anything he wanted. And suddenly we were in business. The dream was coming true. We'd go to Berlin and drink in Nick Cave's bar.

It can't be stated enough that after Katie told me Nick Cave owned a bar in Berlin, and I related this information to Andy, neither of us did any further research or fact-checking. What would that have even been back in the days before we were all perpetually on the internet? Searching Altavista or Yahoo? If we asked Jeeves about Nick Cave owning a Berlin bar and no results showed up, we would simply have assumed that Jeeves was a liar. We didn't know the address or even its name. But we assumed everyone in Germany would. I mean this is Nick Cave we're talking about.

Andy now needed a passport. And to obtain one, first things first, some secondary form of identification. A birth certificate was going to have to do. But we couldn't ask Andy's mom and dad for the original as going on such an adventure was not what they had in mind when they gave Andy the money. Did they know something we didn't? So on the day before my birthday in April we set out for Tewksbury, MA where Andy was born, believing we could procure one there. On the hour-long ride up I-93 we developed an elaborate story to tell the town hall clerk, feeling that not having a birth certificate in the first place was somehow suspect. We decided to say we had driven up from Stratford, CT, *my* hometown, as if the length of our journey would appeal to their sense of kindness and expedite the process. But once inside, Andy panicked and said 'Strathmore', the name of the street our friend Andrew lived on, and not 'Stratford', a town that he'd never been to before. It didn't much matter though as there ended up being no reason to have made the trip at all. The clerk could not help us, and there was another, easier, way to do this, even in that pre-internet age. On the way back, we hit rush-hour traffic and the ride took over three hours. A beginning to my birthday that seemed par for the course. It took another month, and with only days to spare, the passport finally made its way into Andy's hands.

We were set to fly out on June 2nd. Despite our belief in our bad luck, forces conspired to put us on the brink of actually making this happen. Before we could depart, however, there were two pressing matters to attend to. Trashtalk over the previous year had finally culminated in the plans for an Allston (we) vs. JP (Jamaica Plain, they) basketball tournament, to take place on May 31st. Which turned out to be the hottest day of the year. Or at least feel like it. Checking the records now it was 87°, though I remember frequently commenting how it must have been 100. It didn't help that both teams stayed up drinking until 6 AM at a party at the Jamaica Plain house the night before, and the heavy alcohol sweats and unaccustomed exercise seemed to drape further layers of uncomfortable heat over our hungover bodies.

How the rivalry began is lost to the annals of time as these things often are, but looking at the key players it seems to stem from the fact that in Allston, MA – Boston University's student enclave – lies one Pratt Street, on which two years earlier eleven of my friends lived, with only five of them on the lease, some doubling up in closets and storage spaces. In April of that year, I gave myself my first proper mohawk. I always wanted that deep red that Miki from Lush sported back then, but being easily distracted, I bought 'Poppy' because I liked the name, instead of the 'Vampire Red' Manic Panic that was required. This resulted in my hair ending up a disappointing fuchsia. My friend Josh manned the clippers and we left what was shaved off on a metal statue in the small front lawn. By June, birds had worked the hair into a nest. In September, the house was condemned. Pratt continues on, turning into Wadsworth Street, and it was here, on Wads in 1997, that those who later moved to Jamaica Plain had lived. So the territorial rivalry was longstanding. The stakes were high too. If Allston won, Jamaica Plain would then be referred to by all as 'Allston Annex'. The double A having a much better ring to it than us becoming a territory of JP. Which in our minds was never going to happen. Despite the fact that most of our team didn't show up.

JP brought nine players. We had five. Even with the games taking place on Allston turf, the many who said they would play were purposely not answering our calls, Andy included. And this was at a time when we had to walk to a payphone to ring them. With such unevenness, we decided to play four on four, best of seven to eleven, have to win by two. Which meant we had one sub, while the JP side had five. FIVE. A whole other team plus an additional sub!

It was hot. Breathing soon became difficult, scorching lungs unaccustomed to so much usage. I have vivid muscle memories from that day of my throat crackling from inhalations, even more so when I finally drank some water. In line with how much planning I did back then, I did not think to bring any beverages with me. Finally, in desperation after game four, we called a break to head up the hill to Store 24. Desperate gulps and pours of the gallon jug over my head, an aura of woozy red surrounding my upper body as relief sought any nerve endings not already over-occupied with overheated skin and the pain of a too-parched palate being irrigated too late.

Then back to the court. It was pretty even. We were somehow summoning something deep within us, a determination to win rarely shown in our lives at the time. There's a point in every game where it comes down to simply having the will to keep jumping for rebounds. Soon it was all tied up, three games to three, and we were going into the rubber match. Minds long since reduced to mush. Whilst waiting to resume play, crimson bodies deluged with sweat stood hands on hips or pacing tiny circles, attention focused on the monumental effort to get air into lungs that were hours overheated and ready to shut down. Game point keeps changing. Allston up by one. The ball comes to yours truly out by the three point line. A shot I'd only been hitting about 50% all day and warned by my teammates games ago to stop taking. Tension and frustration palpable in the air as feet leave the ground with ball overhead, quickly turning to a drained but triumphant rush as my final fade-away jumper goes in to win it for Allston!

I wasn't used to being this physically exhausted. Which had another drawback in that I wasn't fully prepared for what was coming that evening. It was Lisa's last night in town. She was leaving for Europe the very next day to backpack around with her best friend. And she wasn't returning to Boston afterwards. I was very sad we wouldn't get to spend any more time together. I remember standing wordless in her kitchen, just wanting to savor the last moments. In the state I was in post-basketball court, I was even more ill-equipped than usual to deal with such high emotion. At the time I thought this was just another instance of Life once again throwing me more than I could handle. But there are no accidents. I planned and then played hard those games all the while subconsciously knowing Lisa was leaving that very same day. I set myself up to not feel, and then to be upset about that.

Whatever mechanism I have that automatically blocks such unpleasantness from my consciousness was in full effect. And it seemed like there was nothing I could do about any of it. Why *feel* what's going on and let it get me even more down? My best friend and I were setting out the next morning but one to go drink in Nick Cave's

Berlin bar for nine days. A trip months in the making. Oh sure, we *talked* about how depressed we were and how things never worked out for us. It was practically our m.o. We threw ourselves so deep into that negativity that it couldn't help but manifest in our lives. But there was no question of ever actually dealing with these emotions, even with the prospect looming over our heads – very large and very real –of coming back to our little world being emptier than when we had left it.

This would be different than my last trip to Europe. Andy and I were in complete agreement on the plan – Get Drunk. Talk about Nick Cave. Finding his bar was a foregone conclusion. After all, someone had told me he had one.

III – 'The Road Is Long and The Road Is Hard'

Start as you mean to go on, they say. The entirety of the thing is already contained in the seed itself. That Cave himself fronts The Bad Seeds is perhaps inherently wrapped up in all this. Let me offer a clue of what is to come by telling you that despite living in Boston, Massachusetts, we had bought tickets for a flight leaving from Newark Airport in New Jersey, four-and-a-half hours away. Not directly to Berlin either. No, we'd gotten a great price on flights via LuxAir, Luxembourg's national airline, if we were prepared to have layovers in Luxembourg on each side of the trip. The 'great price' saved us both about $100 a ticket, though in actuality, very little if you factor in the gas, tolls, and parking fees it took to leave from New Jersey. And let's not forget the nine hours travel time to save this tiny amount.

Nevertheless, the prospect of adventure excited us. And so we set off, hopeful young men looking forward to having the time of their lives. Before we even reached the airport, we were beginning to get a sense of how things were going to go. Consulting Andy's diary for the trip, abandoned after only two entries: *It's been difficult. It started in New Jersey where it was unbelievably DIFFICULT to find the parking lot. There was even the threat of having to use a monorail...*

We hadn't left the ground just yet though and once we got drinking, our enthusiasm returned. As we kicked back in the bar, our plane soon taxied into view. Through the gigantic window at the gate we spot 'THE FLYING DREAM' emblazoned on its side. This boded well.

Once on board, however, one of my peculiar habits soon presented itself as a problem. I wanted to get some reading done. Now, Andy and I have always bonded over literature, in fact he is even more of a voracious reader than I. But for a ten-day-long international trip where we were intent on drinking in the style of The Birthday Party and having a great time doing just that, I had brought four novels with me. Short ones, I justified, though being a slow reader, I've rarely ever been able to get through more than one book a week no matter what the size. I was excited to finally start Nabokov's *Transparent Things*, which in *London Fields* Martin Amis calls 'one of the saddest novels in English', quoting its 'Night is always a giant but this one was especially terrible'. There's that Night again. Waiting for me within those pages, that I would of course read but not truly see. In line with this, following back along a metaphysical optometrist's pointing finger, Nabokov's *The Eye* was in my rucksack also. I would take the phrase 'tremulous haloes' from this latter work for the title of a Rockets Burst From The Streetlamps song (page five, 'It was raining as usual, and there were tremulous halos around the streetlamps...' The sentence finishes, unnoticed until now, '...drummed upon by the night.' Curious.)

Terri had been the one to get me back into reading, and I would credit this as to why I also started writing. I loved to read as a child. And let it go during my teenage years except for music magazines. Early on in our friendship she told me 'I just finished William Burroughs *Naked Lunch*, but didn't understand it. You should read it and tell me what happens.' So of course I did. Read it, that is. I couldn't explain anything about the plot, though the penis under the eyelid passage has stayed with me to this day. Next she recommended *Trainspotting*, which I hightailed to the bookstore the morning after seeing said film to procure. And from there I was off. In one of those music magazines, Damon Albarn had spoken of the influence of *London Fields* on Blur's *Parklife* album and, well, that was enough for me to branch out on my own. I loved it. Now, Nabokov was not a stranger to me. See, although I'd stopped reading in high school, I still bought books from time to time. And during my first ever English class at Boston University, a requirement for the business school that I was incongruously attending back then, the professor had us read the first paragraph of Nabokov's *Speak, Memory*. And so impressed was I, that I ran to the BU bookstore immediately after class to purchase this 'autobiography revisited', along with his *Despair*, *The Gift*, and *The Real Life Of Sebastian Knight*. *Lolita* was actually the ninth Nabokov I read. It didn't hold much appeal for me, despite being the classic. But the descriptions on the backsides of these softcover Vintage International editions very much piqued my interest. Me being me, it would take almost four years to get around to reading them. Starting with *Despair* in those post-graduation summer months before setting off for Europe with Terri. Could I really have been receiving such messages about the state of my life from book titles? Next up, later that year at our family Christmas party, Brian of the 1001st cd, also a fellow literature enthusiast, would get me so excited about reading *The Gift* that I stopped drinking mid-soirée and began the arduous task of sobering up so that I could dive into its pages as soon as our guests departed. Enthralled, I finished the novel in four days, staying up long into the night, and, when it felt like I would fall asleep before its final page had passed from right to left hand, I would pull my hair as hard as I could to keep awake. *The Gift* remains the most beautiful novel I have ever read. From that point on, it was all about Nabokov. And by the time these two novels were present in my luggage, I was more than halfway through his literary output.

You'll be pleased to hear too that I didn't stay in business school for long. As winter gave way to spring my sophomore year, I was regularly sleeping until 4 PM, arising to go smoke cigarettes on the benches in front of our dorm before getting some dinner with friends. Registration opened for fall semester and, for a month and a half, I snoozed my way past opening times. When I finally did remember to go to the office, all the management classes I was supposed to take had long been filled up. All was not lost though, as I still had my four electives and - Terri's influence again - I enrolled in an Existentialism class she was taking and three beginner literature courses on my own. By the following semester, I was an English major.

So, back on the plane with Andy, and I'm getting ready to tuck into *Transparent Things*, quite oblivious to leaving my friend, who has never been out of the country before and has spent a lot of money to do so, to go on an adventure with me, on his own. In order to get some reading done. So that I wouldn't 'seem like a jerk', I conceded to keep drinking with him, which in my mind was rather big of me as I just wanted uninterrupted time with Nabokov's prose. These hours that I saw offered before me to spend with a book in my hands were somehow different from the time I had to do so at home. Which was all the time, whenever I wasn't working or drinking. I think Andy was more in tune with the idea of how things begin giving a good indication of how they would continue, and was concerned that I might spend our entire vacation together with my nose in a novel. Whereas this concept never occurred to me. The world – like The Birthday Party song – was wild. And so, in my mind, things just happen, and me acting like a selfish ass at the beginning of our trip in no way implied that I would at any other point in time.

Flight attendants soon start serving brandy and, eventually, I put Nabokov down. Directly in front of us sits a man who doesn't speak any English but is, nevertheless, ordering aperitifs at double our already alarming drinking pace. He is soon cut off, and not happy about this. Angry shouting leads to him soon standing and screaming at a stewardess, and for some moments we genuinely feel our flight might be turned around for safety's sake, the trip abandoned before we even reach foreign soil. Things eventually calm down, but sleep and quality literature time just aren't going to happen. Perhaps it was because of the atmosphere I was attempting to read it in, but I remember one thing and one thing only from *Transparent Things* - that Nabokov uses the phrase 'Cunning Stunts' as the title of a play. A quick internet search reveals I'm not alone in these two words obliterating any other memory of the book. And I've always found this quite out of character for him, an author so careful never to use a curse word.

We arrive at Luxembourg airport at 6:30 AM after drinking for a good seven hours on the plane. By 7 AM we realize the bar is open and will take American money. With nothing else to do as we wait through our six-hour layover, we begin drinking in earnest. None of this 'I'm trying to read' or 'maybe I'll get some sleep'. Things are serious now, our mission has begun.

The tables in the bar are tiny and every eight beers we have to move as the empty bottles and overflowing ashtrays preclude anything else being placed upon them. Dirty, or rather just shocked, looks from passersby mean we switch to an area on the opposite side of the room to begin again, hoping our trail won't prevent us from being able to procure more refreshments from the bar. Andy's diary recounts two Frenchmen wanting to beat us up for being obnoxious drunk Americans at 9 AM but I have little recollection of this. The diary also states that we drank fourteen beers in three hours. Given our drinking capacity at the time, this doesn't seem like all that much to me. A year later, when Andy and I lived together, he found it necessary to impose a 'fifteen drink cap' on his nightly intake. And true to his word, he never let himself imbibe more than fifteen large Tanqueray and tonics on any given evening. Fourteen bottles in three hours this Luxembourg morning, but we are here for six. Twenty eight beers seems more appropriate for our total airport intake. And this after drinking beer and brandy for seven hours on the plane with no sleep.

We eventually move closer to the gate and while away the remaining time betting on the Arrivals/Departures board. True to our joy-in-sabotage natures, we aren't betting on which flight will arrive first. No, which plane will be delayed next and for how long is what occupies our interest. Our own flight to Berlin, however, is right on time.

We stroll out on the tarmac, each very, very intoxicated, and are confronted with a twenty six person propeller plane. One without even a name shining off its side like The Flying Dream. I stop in my tracks. 'I can't do this.' Andy reassuring me, 'Don't worry, the pilot is Han Solo.'

I step forward, stumbling into the tiny interior and collapsing, disgustingly drunken, into my seat. The ride is disorientating, to say the least. I'm convinced we are upside-down at one point. My innards certainly feel such effects, taking well into the next day to recover. As I sit spinning through the liminal state between sleeping and waking, curled up in a protective ball in an effort to make it all stop, I occasionally peek out from the maelstrom to spy Andy alert and beatific, sipping champagne with a rakish gleam in his eye.

We touch down at Tempelhof at 1:40 PM, not nearly enough time to recover from putting my body through roughly twenty-one hours travel time and as many drinks to match. But we are here! Time to find Nick Cave's bar and get to it. The peculiar sensation I feel as we step out into the afternoon sun has stayed with me over the years. A curious mixture of wide-open possibility, joy and satisfaction that something we desired was coming true, coupled with an absolutely appalling alcohol-sweat-soaked exhaustion.

My mother kindly booked us a hotel room for the first and last nights of the trip. The travel agent assuring us it is right in the center of Berlin. It very much is not. We exchange some money and, hailing a cab, are shocked as the city sights zip past while we seem headed out into the countryside. Even more aghast when we are presented with the fare, equivalent to 50 American dollars. Andy has only brought $100 with him, while I'm starting the trip with close to $300. Our very first excursion - away from everything, mind you - is taking a good cut out of this.

We find ourselves in Biesdorf, checking in to Hotel K on Kopenicker Strasse, 'nick' right there in the street name, along with the 'kope' of another of my favourite songwriters. The clerk at the desk confirms that yes, we are very far away from everything. It is getting towards evening now and perhaps the best thing to do is get some sleep in order to start fresh in the morning. Andy informing me he'll need to drink more before bedtime and so we set off for the shops, buying sixteen cans of German lager. Soon settling into the hotel room for the night, me barely finishing two beers as I once again unsuccessfully try to get some reading done. Falling asleep early to the sounds of German television, leaving Andy to polish off six cans.

Morning comes and we are up and ready to take on Berlin. This is going to involve catching a train back into the city, and walking to the station carrying all our luggage as well as the eight remaining sixteen-ounce cans proves too difficult. We spend a good deal of time debating the financial as well as spiritual dilemma of what it would mean to actually jettison alcohol. Finally stashing the beer behind some bushes with a vague plan to come back for it later, or if not, we can take solace in the good karma it will bestow upon us if found by some teenagers in need. Back in the States later that summer, relating the trip to my cousins, they chastise me, groaning 'Ooooo, never throw away good alcohol! Get rid of your shirts or something.' It is a 45 minute train journey back to Berlin proper, our destination Rosenthaler Platz and the Circus Hostel where Katie and Paul had worked. We're hoping that dropping their names will at least get us some free drinks. We're never heading back to Biesdorf for those cans.

It is Friday at the start of summer in a major European capital, prime vacation time, and of course we haven't booked ahead. Amazingly though, Good Fortune is shining down upon us and we are able to procure a room for not only tonight but the following evening as well. I immediately ask the young man behind the reception desk 'Do you know Nick Cave?' A formality really, everyone must know Nick Cave, but this is friendlier than simply demanding directions to his bar. A look of confusion follows, which will come to be the norm with this line of questioning. He seems to think I mean does he know

Nick Cave personally. I clarify. Our receptionist knows of him, but no, he doesn't know where this bar is. 'Berlin is a big city though', he humbly offers and I refuse to be the slightest bit deterred from our mission.

Dropping off our belongings, it occurs to us that maybe we should attempt to continue in a more practical manner. We haven't even brought a travel guide with us, so obtaining one becomes the first order of business. There might even be a mention of Nick Cave's bar in the *Rough Guide To Berlin*. We'll have to read closely though, we don't even know the name of this establishment, and it is possible that it isn't simply called 'Nick Cave's Bar'. We set out for a multi-leveled bookstore in Alexanderplatz, which holds the promise of an English-language section. After asking a number of clerks if they speak our language, we are now patiently waiting for a promised employee who does 'speak a little' English. A middle-aged woman finally approaching us, very kind, smiling, wishing to be helpful. 'Hello, I speak English.' More smiles as she continues, 'How can you help me?'

I smile back, letting out a little laugh, thinking she is having a little joke with her word order. Only she isn't.

Consulting Andy's diary again: *At this point I want to state for the record that no one here speaks English but everyone says they can speak 'a little'. It's like when people say they can get you LSD because they don't want to be someone who can't and they string you along for a week or so with empty promises. This is what Germans who can speak 'a little' English do. They lead you around their neighborhood or store in circles instead of just admitting that they have no idea what you're talking about and can't help you at all. They don't even refrigerate their soda and they all drink FANTA© for some reason. They even sell it at Burger King, FANTA.*

This well-meaning woman doesn't know where Nick Cave's bar is either. We buy the English edition of *Let's Go Berlin*, considering it very wise of us, and go to eat for the first time that day. At Burger King. We are indeed amazed that Fanta is one of the main beverages on offer and are quite tickled with the German pronunciation of it – 'fahn-tuh'. En route to BK, we begin to notice posters featuring a close-up of a woman in a red one-piece bathing suit on a beach holding up a fork on which is pierced a large sausage. The caption reads 'HOT DAYS HOT NIGHTS'. These are soon appearing everywhere, all over the city, in direct contrast to our own experience. We don't know what to make of this ad campaign or even what it is for, though this commercialized cognitive dissonance seems emblematic of the strange space we now find ourselves in. Other people our age, heck, other people in general, just like to have a good time - 'fun', as it is known. They aren't overly drawn to darkly romantic lyrics, certainly aren't inspired by them to fly halfway across the world to revel in debauchery. Perusing our newly acquired guidebook, I make a note of Freak Out Records that I wouldn't mind visiting. Maybe we'll have time to do something else this trip besides drink in Nick Cave's bar. Discussion turning to how awesome an international inventory of record stores would be, entitled, of course, *Let's Go Rock!* And even more useful, a guide to all the bar scenes, *Let's Go Drink!* Andy then hitting upon the genius idea of combining the two as *Let's Go Bankrupt!* That the internet would soon make such printed material all but obsolete would have blown our ramblin' Fanta-soaked minds.

We soon head back to the hostel, more specifically the hostel bar, pulling up two stools to the bar itself. Andy telling me to play it cool, that we'll mention I know Katie and Paul in due time. We can't reveal this card too early, there are free drinks on the line. And so we settle in for the rest of the night. Which is what one does on their first real evening visiting a major European capital for the first time. There might be centuries of culture out there and other less high-minded avenues of delight to take in, but instead we sit in this dark room for hours, sincerely believing we stand a good chance of being on the receiving end of a free beer or two. Besides, Katie and Paul had lit the fuse on this whole trip to begin with via that off-handed comment in Spain nine months earlier. It seems only right to begin on their trail. It transpires that the man behind the bar is the fella who had taught Paul to play chess. I compliment him on how impressed I had been with Paul's pawn game back in Barcelona. Still no offers of a round on the house though. And as the hours wear on, these never come. I don't know how long we are here but I measure the evening in what we imbibed. Ten beers and two shots of Jägermeister a piece.

As closing time rings out, around 1 AM, a pretty blonde Scottish girl strides in. 'Choo-Choo! Choo-Choo!' Raising her right arm, bent 90 degrees at the elbow, and repeatedly yanking it down like a conductor pulling a whistle. 'Choo-Choo! Choo-Choo!' Andy and I are most amused.

'Why are you acting like a train?'

'Choo-Choo!' comes the response.

With the bar now shut, we follow her out the door, where luckily she is going our way into the hostel proper.

Up the stairs and into the lobby by the reception desk, where we meet a ragtag assembly of fellow travelers. Choo-Choo Girl eventually relinquishing her railway impersonation to introduce herself as Eirin from Dundee, following the Scottish national football team around with her best friend Hanna. There's the Americans Susan and Mike, and a few other shadowy figures lurking in the lobby, ethereal beings whose presence seems par for the course for what happens next. Andy and I revealing our mission to the group and although none have come across Nick Cave's bar during their time in Berlin, they all find it a noble pursuit. When Mike, however, tells me that he thinks Nick Cave is only 'alright' and that he himself is a Dave Matthews fan, it really opens my eyes as to how others might live. But this man has just returned from the Czech Republic and after an hour or so he disappears, returning to the jovial getting-to-know-each-other atmosphere with a bottle of absinthe. Andy and I have of course heard rumours of the green fairy's charms but to behold her in person is something we've only ever dreamed of, never thinking we'd actually see the day. For back then, absinthe was only legally available in the Czech Republic and Portugal. Even in these locales, in compliance with their laws, bars could only serve you two shots, as after four you would start hallucinating. This was the muse that sent the poets mad. And we are very excited to be making her acquaintance.

Let me remind you that we had just consumed ten beers and two shots of Jäger each at the hostel bar, and are now presently reclining in the lounge with further cans. Out come the glasses and the sugar to begin the absinthe ritual. Of which we gladly partake for the three rounds that are poured. In between, and in addition to these, Andy and I are also grabbing the bottle and swigging freely, long deep gulps. I reckon six shots total went down my throat. I don't reckon much else after that.

IV – 'The Time Of Our Great Undoing'

When people tell you what not to do with Absinthe, pay attention to them. They are not making up rules for no reason. They just don't want your death on their hands. The fact that we are both able to walk and think amazes me to this day. – from Andy's diary

I wake up at 9:30 the next night and walking down the street to Burger King is the hardest thing I've ever had to do in my life. We are both to hallucinate for two-and-a-half days afterwards.

The diary continues: *People moved out and then into our hostel room and we could not get out of bed. The people who moved in returned from a whole day of exploring Berlin and we still could not get out of our beds. Both of us are blatantly hallucinating and I can't really feel that much of my body. We broke the rules of absinthe and now we are 'poor bastards'.*

I am back in bed by 11 PM. Being awake for more than an hour and a half is more than I can bear. Andy decides to drink through it.

Aug went back to bed and I was sitting in an alley about 50 ft. away from the door of our hostel when the girls Hanna and 'Mock Lisa' (our name for Eirin, who bore more than a passing resemblance to the recipient of my half-dozen mix tapes) *found me and immediately recognized that I needed beer quickly or I may never return to normal. Sure enough after about six beers I have begun to feel human again and can somewhat ignore the hallucinogenic effects of the absinthe hangover. I managed to wake Aug up at about 1 AM after a strange confrontational incident occurred between Hanna, I, our 'crew', and the man at the hostel desk who tried to prevent us from being sold more beer.*

Andy wakes me up, more pleased than I have ever seen him. He's positively triumphant and can't wait to tell me this story and show off their bounty. It is a struggle, however, as I am resisting getting out of bed with all my bludgeoned being. I am listening though, perhaps from residual guilt for trying to read on the plane instead of hanging out, or the knowledge that it is Saturday night in Berlin and we've just met these two really cool attractive girls who are still here. But fighting against this is an almighty urge to sleep, a martial law imperative imposed by my brain amidst the chaos of still processing what had happened the night before, knowing that I need much more recovery time and possibly a hospital. But what's the only thing that could prove victorious in the face of all this? What does Aug Stone hold dear above all? That's right - Love.

I manage to get up only to collapse against the doorjamb to our shared room, the magnetic pull back to my welcoming bed still incredibly strong. Whereupon Andy fires off the magic words. 'Aug, I'm in love with Hanna. I've never met a woman who could drink with me all night like this before.' And with that I grab my shoes and follow him down to the hostel lobby.

Andy's story that he's been dying to tell me, and by rights is quite proud of, is that the midnight merriment in the lounge had gotten quite out of hand, culminating in the receptionist forbidding them from bringing any more beer in from the hostel bar. Annoyed yet in control of the situation, Andy and another man proceeded to slip outside and find the nearest döner kebab stand. Emptying all the deutsche marks in his pocket onto the counter, Andy instructed, 'Beer. As much as this will buy.' And the two returned to the hostel carrying 35 large lagers.

Making my way past scowls at the reception desk into the lounge, the air still tight with tension, I sink into a sofa, cracking open a contraband can. Everyone seems genuinely sympathetic to the damage Andy and I inflicted on ourselves the night before. Mike and his absinthe bottle now long gone. Eirin and Hanna are heading to Prague the next day to watch Scotland play the Czech Republic. Things start to look up as they invite us to come with them, giving us each handwritten notes with the info for The Clown & Bard youth hostel. This is certainly a change in our luck. We might just be able to crawl out of this absinthe hangover hellhole and spend a few days with two awesome women in yet another foreign country, maybe even making it back in time to get some serious drinking done in Nick Cave's bar at the end of the trip. The girls are catching an early morning train so we soon say goodnight and goodbye, all hugs and smiles. We would meet them in Prague soon enough.

There is only one problem with this plan – it is day three of our trip and Andy has run out of money. I have a couple of traveler's checks that nonetheless will not cover a sidetrip to Prague and keep us drinking, eating, and having a place to crash for the remainder of our stay. I do, however, have a credit card. One that I have only ever used once before. My mother had always done her best to instill in me the principle of never going into debt and I took this seriously. The only time I had ever used the card was the day after my 1000th cd party to buy twelve further cds. One of which was Nick Cave's *From Her To Eternity*. I am still pleased with this synchronicity.

Andy and I continue drinking in the lounge with some other latenighters. There are, after all, 35 cans to get through. We discuss the problem. I will do what I can to make it happen for my friend. But I don't want to go into too much debt. I announce we will save money by taking the bus. This suggestion immediately bringing worried looks from those assembled around us. 'Have you ever been on the roads in the Czech Republic? You don't want to take a bus over those.' Nevertheless, I stay firm on this.

Given that we hallucinated for two-and-a-half days after the absinthe – we didn't imagine Eirin and Hanna, I assure you, we met them right before the bottle appeared, just in the nick of time – and that we were naturally night owls anyway, the order of events the following morning are a little hazy.

I have a strong recollection of waking up and seeing a woman sitting on one of the far beds in our hostel room, her head in her hands. Her boyfriend eventually walks in and they soon leave. Andy returning to the room shortly after, informing me that my intense snoring had caused this couple great distress, that she had even been screaming at me to stop in the early hours, to no avail. At first I thought this couldn't be, what kept them awake might have been the Jesus & Mary Chain bootleg– Milan

1989 – that I had fallen asleep blaring on my Walkman, its chaotic feedback echoing so perfectly the noise in my soul. But as a precaution pre-shouting, Andy had removed my headphones and pressed STOP. On the Walkman that is, not my soul. The couple's vexation wasn't just about the music, it was mainly due to my most unmelodic cacophonous nasal tissue. I felt great shame that I disrupted their vacation and sleep, but what was I to do? I had nearly died drinking absinthe. Come to think of it, this must've happened the day before, the morning directly after the green hell fiasco. At which point I then fell promptly back asleep until 9:30 PM.

So the Sunday we are due to leave Circus Hostel and make our way to Prague then, is the morning I am waiting patiently for Andy to wake up to make our noontime check-out. As I do so, I hear him say, to no one in particular, 'Take me to the Egg Hospital!' and then turn back over into his pillow.

Eventually, we are up and out, en route to the bus station. I'm still hoping tickets will be cheap enough that I can pay with the cash I have on hand and keep us in good spirits for the rest of our trip. It doesn't take us long to reach the depot. It takes even less time to find out that buses do not run from Berlin on Sundays. Though it does take quite a while for the full impact of this to sink in.

I don't know why we didn't immediately get on a train. Again, our physical and mental states at this point are still very altered and very damaged. Our psyches aswirl with hallucinations, vying for attention with the extreme sense that something is not right with our bodies, and to please do something about this.

What we do do is go in search of Freak Out Records. Which takes rather a long time to locate. And is, of course, closed on Sunday.

Making our way back to a new hostel, we buy some exotic beers and head to a nearby park to assess the situation. I don't know if you've ever sat drinking strawberry-flavoured beer watching children play basketball on a dreary Sunday afternoon while the possibility of a great new romantic adventure is now hundreds of miles away in another foreign capital and you're not sure how you're going to get there, let alone take another couple steps without collapsing into much-needed recovery sleep in order to assuage your mother-of-all hangovers and shut out its bizarre psychedelic effects, but let me tell you I do not recommend it. It is one of the lowest points of my life. We are in bed by 7:30 PM.

V – 'The Air Is Full Of Promises'

'NA-NA-NAAA NA-NA-NAAA NA-NA-NAAA-NA-NA-NAAA NA-NAAAAAA'

We're on the train! Accompanied by what seem like thousands of Scottish football fans roaring this chant at the top of their lungs. You can't help but get wrapped up in the excitement. Even I put my book down and join in the jovial atmosphere. These madmen and women have been drinking heavily since 8 AM, en route to see Scotland play the Czech Republic in a Euro 2000 qualifying match at Prague's Letenský Stadion in two days time. Where Hanna and Eirin will be. At every stop in Deutschland, beers in hand, these amped-up Scots cram as many heads as they can fit out train windows to shout at innocent faces that they had just 'destroyed' Germany in their last match. Referring, of course, to Scotland's 1-nil Friendly victory back in April, over a month ago.

It is only much later that I discover what it is they are actually singing. Indulging my Britpop obsession one day at the Import section of Newbury Comics, without Lisa there to persuade me otherwise, I purchase Fat Les' 'Vindaloo' single, knowing this fictional band to be a side project of Blur bassist, Alex James. I pop the CD into my car stereo and, to my delighted surprise and horror, on comes the 1998 English World Cup Song. Even more than a year after our return home, I am still shellshocked enough from our European excursion to have hearing this familiar nonsense bring rushing back ghosts of hangovers most foul coupled with a strange nostalgic joy as I race through the streets of Allston to share my discovery with Andy.

Love is proving an even more motivating force than Nick Cave. We are up early, having gone so far as to actually find out the train schedule ahead of time. Unheard of for two men who hadn't bothered to check if Nick Cave really did own a bar in Berlin. And although we've only been in the country for three days, and most of that spent drunk and hallucinating, Andy seems to be picking up the language. Twenty years later, I can still hear his reprimanding tones sonorously ring out as I try to pull open a door – '*Drücken*, **Push**, fool!' His subconscious also continuing to be a wonderfully fertile ground for hilarity, with him relating to me a dream he'd had the previous night about a special 'Condom Episode' of *The Brady Bunch* that, unaired at the time, was finally seeing the light of day. Describing multiple arty camera angles, mostly shot in their backyard or through windows into the house, Andy's retelling making me feel as if I am watching it myself. Though, as such is the language of dreams, the visions soon shift until simultaneously dissipating and falling apart. Any possible reconstruction of the plot even by the next day would be as much of a wild goose chase as the one we are currently on. Scant details remain - Alice was a major player, but the condom was all Bobby's. However, with the whole crew gathered together at episode's end in their familiar front room, heads shook in mirthful reproach as the family delivered the punchline in unison - 'looks like Dad forgot to put on the condom again!'

As the railside signs start to read 'Praha', and our train speeds ever nearer, we begin to feel actually good about things, moreso than I can recall in quite a while. With so much merriment surrounding us, it can't help but rub off, doing wonders to allay the remnants of the absinthe hangovers still kicking our bloodstreams and synapses whilst smudging our spiritual auras. Clutching the Clown & Bard brochure - on which Eirin had jotted us a note in that alluring, carefree, girls' handwriting - with the highest of hopes. We keep referring to the hostel as The Clown & Barrel, perhaps indicative of everything surrounding the trip, nay, our lives, thus far. What happened next should have at least put us on our guard.

Descending from the train and out onto the streets of Prague, we immediately came face to fists with three pre-teen skinhead boys, sporting leather jackets with no shirts underneath, beating the absolute fuck out of a payphone with their bare knuckles. Luckily they pay us no mind, scrambling to get ahead of each other and deliver more wild yet precise blows, raining these down upon the poor machine until it comes crashing off its supporting wall. Out pours a waterfall of coin like a Vegas slot machine. With lightning fast agility, they scoop everything up into arms and pockets before bolting from the scene. The sheer speed and violence of it all is downright ugly, not to mention disconcerting.

Shaken by this first impression and not quite sure where to go, it being 3 PM, we decide to duck into a nearby bar for our first meal of the day, fantastic grilled cheese sandwiches, and some further refreshment, of course. We are never to come across this establishment again though I am constantly on the look-out for a way back, so good is the grilled cheese. We sit atop stools at the counter speaking openly of how such an aggressive display with the payphone has left us feeling physically sick. Taking the time to calm down and regroup, we soon get our bearings and head up a hill to where the hostel is marked on our map. I point out the hill because it really does feel like a trek. The heat hanging heavy this June afternoon, not helping the fact that we'd skipped morning ablutions in order to get to the station on time. We've also just been drinking for five hours.

Sweaty and tired, we arrive at The Clown & Bard's doors. It is one of those moments you replay over and over again in your mind, a split-second you fervently wish you could have back to choose again, choose differently. Vivid is my recollection of walking into the reception area and seeing Eirin laughing in the bar behind, not twenty feet away. Andy, being particularly aware of his own dishevelment, staying back in the shadows of the entranceway. There is no room at the inn. The man at the desk is kind and patient but firm on this. He will, however, do his best to locate us two beds nearby and quickly picks up a phone. I go back to Andy and explain the situation. 'Do you see Eirin over in the bar? Let's tell her what's going on, have a drink, and then we can go drop our stuff off at this other hostel.'

Andy, however, does not feel this is the best course of action. 'I can't face them right now. It's hot, I haven't showered, I've been drinking all day.' The emphasis he puts on the final words clearly communicating, from somewhat of a high horse, that he considers himself to be in much worse shape than I. That he, of course, has consumed far more than I have on the train. This is true, it took me an hour or two to finally put the book down. Andy continues, 'Let's just go drop our stuff off and shower at the other place. We'll be back in like half an hour.' Famous last words.

The receptionist informing us that right down the street is another private hostel with two beds awaiting us for the night. We pick up our rucksacks and head out, delusionally believing that upon our return all will still be as it is now. Have we learned nothing from the changing nature of our absinthe hallucinations? We shower, and my goodness does it feel amazing, then take a little more time to make ourselves presentable with what little we have in our luggage. Striding back to The Clown & Bard, giant hopeful steps, still referring to it as The Clown & Barrel. Looking now at the note Hanna gave Andy, no wonder we called it such. She had spelt it 'The Clown & Barred'. Perhaps that should have offered a clue.

'The blonde Scottish girl who was here half an hour ago, where is she?'

'I don't know who you're talking about, sir.'

'We were here not half an hour ago and there was a blonde Scottish girl drinking in the bar. Do you know who she is?'

'We have many guests here, sir.'

I'm getting frazzled. 'Her name is Eirin, she's traveling with her friend Hanna. They've come to watch the Scotland Czech Republic match. They arrived yesterday. Can you tell us what room they're in? Or can we at least leave a message for them?'

I told you this man was kind and patient. I watch him earnestly scan the guest book, wanting to help us out, and even though his eyes as they glance up to meet mine betray the sadness that is coming, I catch no early warning. 'I'm sorry, sir. There is no one here by those names.'

Andy and I look at each other, panicked. This can't be happening.

'You found other rooms for us. Maybe they couldn't get a room either and you found them someplace else to stay?'

'I don't recall anyone with those names, or two Scottish women. It could have been my colleague who dealt with them yesterday...'

'Can you phone him?'

'I'm afraid not, sir. It's his day off.'

'But...' But...but...but....!!!

'There are many Scottish fans here, sir. Perhaps they met up with friends who found them other lodging...'
My face betraying complete and utter disbelief.

'I'm sorry, sir.'

'That's what happens when you try,' Andy pronounces as we settle into a table at the hostel bar, our plan being to simply wait until they come back. If they were here earlier, they might very well return. And we have no better options. It isn't like there is a whole new beautiful gothic city out there to explore or anything...

VI – 'All Drunk And Howling At The Moon'

It is early evening and the bar is quite empty. We start in on the local lager until I remember a story my grandmother once told me. A month after I was born, my grandparents embarked on a three-week guided tour of the Communist Bloc. Of Russian and Polish descent, it would be seeing where their parents had come from. My grandmother's mother, whom she referred to as 'The Old Battle Axe', always sounded to me like an amazing woman. No-nonsense, spoke eleven languages, a phenomenal cook, escaped Russia around 1900 to settle in suburban Pennsylvania and run three boarding houses. Having come to America for a reason, she never spoke about her homeland. On this trip behind the 'Iron Curtain', my grandmother, Anne, is held at the Russian border for hours over the matter of her passport reading her birth name, Mary-Anne. They almost don't let her go. When upon returning she tells her mother of this horrific scene, The Old Battle Axe's response is simply 'Serves you right. You had no business going back there.' But my grandmother is eventually released, and a few days later, in what was then Czechoslovakia, the tour guide treats them all to a Czech national spirit, Slivovitz. Which my grandmother loved. I can still remember her smile of pure delight as she would mime sipping it, and asking for another. But when ordering a third, the tour guide cut her off, warning against excess with this potent plum liqueur.

I spy the Slivovitz sign at the bar, relate this story to Andy, and go to get us shots. We toast my grandmother and down the amber spirits, at which point I promptly stand up, walk to the restroom, and vomit copiously into a urinal. Which seems a pretty good metaphor for where we are at in our lives.

Spewing like this is also odd on two accounts. Firstly, over the course of my sixteen-year drinking career, there has only been one other beverage that my bloodstream immediately refused entry. One evening two years previous, I had been sitting on a floor with some friends doing shots of Southern Comfort. A young lady I was fooling around with at the time strolled into the room, perched herself in a chair above me, and soon felt I wasn't paying enough attention to her. As the next shot slid down my throat, she cocked her leg back and kicked me in the face. Hard. I have never been able to imbibe SoCo since, even its scent brings back a sensation of nauseous pain. Also during those sixteen years, I only ever threw up about a dozen times. I never had much trouble keeping it all down, despite many a night when that might have preempted a mighty hangover.

So I'm quite thrown by the experience of my body rejecting the Slivovitz like this in such an unpleasant manner. I grab a beer to gargle away the taste of vomit. I can't go back to our hostel to brush my teeth, we have beverages to drink here. And women to wait for. We put in long hours that night, staying until closing time, to no avail.

With nothing else to do, we while away the time writing postcards to the folks back home. There is one particular house we had befriended on our nightly walks back from The Model. Taking a different route one night in order to stop at Natalie's Pizza on Commonwealth Ave., I hit upon the ingenious idea that there might be perfectly good food in the trash bins behind, and indeed the same for the Dunkin' Donuts a little down the road. Finding the idea more hilarious than practical, I grabbed a black bag, began to drag it with us, and before long we came across some latenighters sitting on their Linden Street porch at 3 AM. We told them of our bounty and opened up the bag only to be proved wrong about anything edible inside, such as there was being covered with coffee grinds and actual garbage. We then proceeded to strike up a conversation with these friendly chaps. Hereafter, once a week or so, we'd alter our post-bar course to see if they were still up – a pleasant break from watching the Nick Cave video collection – and hang out on their front steps until nearly sunrise conversing about music, literature, and Life.

Our postcard to them is of high priority. We had told them of our plans to find Nick Cave's bar and they were very supportive of such a venture. Andy and I spend a long time considering our words as we pass the card back and forth, alternately composing each sentence. When all available space has been filled, we sit back to consider what we are viewing as a masterpiece. 'Scottish Women!' one line reads, for we had not yet given up hope. 'Egg Hospitals!' comes the next. In the years since, I have often wished I had copied our words into a notebook of my own. I knew them to be a communication from my very soul. The only other line I can recall - one of mine - seemed particularly poetic at the time - 'Love is a two-way street but people in England drive on the other side of the road.' Only about half the ink filling up this 4"X6" card has anything to do with our actual trip. But we know they will understand.

The bar at The Clown & Bard is closing up for the night and the ladies have not returned. I, being tired and still tasting of plum puke, am anxious to get some sleep. Despite the hilarity of writing up our misadventures for those back home, misery is once again peeking its mischievous head around the corner at these two easy targets slowly emerging from an absinthe hangover. Andy, quite rightly, points out 'how often are we in Prague?' and that we should go live it up. Which involves finding the only other bar that is open in the area at this time of night and watching Eastern Europe ice hockey on a tiny television with a handful of other degenerates trying to make the most of their Tuesday 3 AM. A long-haired heavy metal-looking dude looks like he might be cool to befriend but he ends up not speaking any English. He is anyways soon making out with the one female in the place then getting into a half-hearted fistfight with some other patrons before finally being ejected from the premises. Violence is still in the air. And tension creeping into Andy and my relationship as the hardship of it all is beginning to sink in. Out of the absinthe into another abyss. By 4 AM I am in a full-on sulk demanding we go back to the hostel. Andy countering that we will, as soon as we each finish one more round. Which I am physically incapable of swallowing at this point. Sensing this, Andy insists on these conditions, knowing they will keep us out later. The longer I go without touching my beer, the more he can imbibe.

After a few hours sleep, we have to be up to switch hostels, for ours is full on the eve of the football match.

The thousands of Scots invading the city have booked most of the city's cheap lodging but our current location again help us locate a room down the street, one where all six beds are pushed up against each other. I snap at Andy, 'If we're going to be sleeping this close together, I don't want you fucking me in the middle of the night.' Dark laughter. Andy hopping back into bed, something I crave but instead it is up to me to go cash the traveler's checks in order to keep us alive and drinking.

The American Express office is over the hills and three miles away in the city center. It feels good to be up and out and on my own. I convert the checks into Czech koruna and it seems like we'll have enough money to get through the rest of the trip. Excited to find a record store in a little mall on Václavské nám., one of Prague's main strips, once inside and perusing the 'C' section, the sight of Nick Cave & The Bad Seeds' *Kicking Against The Pricks* arrests my heart and freezes my flipping fingers. Its presence is discombobulating. I can't wrap my head around it. Why would the covers album be the only Bad Seeds anyone would have in their shop? In this magical medieval city, where Rabbi Löwe once worked wonders, it must be some sort of sign. Löwe had even fashioned the famous Golem of Prague, named Josef, a name Cave himself was fond of using - 'Knockin' On Joe', 'I Had A Dream, Joe', and here, on this very disc, his version of 'Hey Joe'.

Personally, I have always been fond of the album's finale, 'The Carnival Is Over'. Was that the message? A harbinger of present and future hopes dashed? A year later I will put this song on the car stereo for Andy as we drive away from saying goodbye to the last of our female friends now leaving us all alone in Allston. But here and now in Prague, the awaiting communication, if in fact it can be understood at all, kicks against my brain, all too much for my fragile being to bear.

Some lunch is in order and a pizza place soon comes into view halfway up the hill on my return journey. What could lay in wait there for a non-Slavic-speaking vegetarian? The waitress is most kind, with a good grasp of English, but I'm not sure it is in the Czech psyche to not feature meat in every dish. For although I've now made it through the absinthe hallucinations, the pizza I order seems to contain at least three varieties of sausage masquerading as mushrooms.

Arriving back at the hostel at 3 PM, I hope to share and thus allay some of my distress about *Kicking Against The Pricks* being the only Cave in town. I mean you wouldn't choose that as your sole Bad Seeds album, would you?

I walk into our room, still dark with the shades drawn. The figure in Andy's bed stirring slightly.

'Just a small handful of donuts.'

Assuming he must be rising through the depths of slumber and wanting breakfast, I ask, 'What?'

'Fuck you, I know what I said.'

This animosity setting the tone for the day. Andy doesn't seem to think the lone presence of *Kicking Against The*

Pricks is as big a spiritual deal as I, so I drag him down to Václavské nám. to see for himself. At which he shrugs. I fume with rage that no one sees my point, or rather that no one will admit to seeing it, for surely this is obvious. *Kicking Against The Pricks* had come out in 1986, thirteen years earlier, while *The Best Of* has just been released. Why wouldn't they have the newer one in stock? Unless popular demand is so great the shop can't keep up with the discs flying off the shelves? A possibility, and largely a moot point as I own them all anyway and am not going to be purchasing any doubles on this trip. But the matter still weighs heavily upon me.

As we wander through the city's public squares, we see hundreds of Scottish fans – kicking balls around, drinking heavily, one even lifting up a kilt in ecstatic joy at a goal scored. Let me tell you this is the last thing you want to see when you're hungover, miserable, and, in every sense of the word, lost. A multitude of Scots, proliferating through the streets, yet not the two we hope to find. Andy and my mutual bitchiness becoming quite entertaining as we settle into it. Me finding it necessary to stay conscious of how much money we have, along with things like check-out times and train departures, while Andy possesses a certain lightness of being, the kind of freedom that comes from non-attachment to such matters, perhaps a prerequisite to the pursuit of 'a good time'. At some point during our perambulations, I propose renting a boat and heading out on the Charles River.

'Why would we want to do that?'

'It might be fun. We could drink.'

'Yeah, anything's fun when you're drinking,' Andy counters in a manner that manages to both agree with me and also shoot down my suggestion as if it is the single stupidest thing he's ever heard in his life. His tone so searing as to still be burned into my brain twenty years later. Neither do I forget his words, a sort of mantra I will use many times in the coming years as a guiding light to ward off boredom.

Andy taking to periodically asking me, 'Aug, where's Hanna?' Mirth and despair co-mingling uneasily with futility. The realization that we might very well never find them again sinks in deep. And for young men accustomed to heartbreak, it is the initial hope that makes it so much more the worse. Prague with all its gorgeousness and ethereal vibes of History lay before us. At odds with our diary entry - *There really is nothing to do in Europe but smoke cigarettes and fall in love.*

We walk on into the night and soon it begins to rain. I have a vivid memory of Andy hanging over a parapet above the city, genius and devilment dancing together in his expression as he asks 'have we checked to see the rain isn't just beer yet?' Opening his mouth wide to wildly shake his upturned face back and forth in the downpour. A smile, a laugh, and then eyes close for a moment of peace before the true storm is unleashed. Bellowing out into the night 'Knockin' Onnnnnnn Praaaaaa-haaaaa'. Its full-bodied tones descending over the city below, a nighttime enchantment for something unknowable at heart. Andy continuing to let loose this variation on the Bad Seeds' 'Knockin' On Joe', much to his own amusement, and it must be said, although I want nothing more at this point than to descend into the arms of sleep, also to mine.

We eventually make it back to the city center and duck out of the spitting heavens into a sports bar. Anything's fun when you're drinking. Andy showing no signs of wanting to stop any time soon. At one point I turn to him and spout, 'Maybe I don't want to have any fun. Maybe I don't want to be like you.'

Again compromises are reached and we stay in that empty saloon until we soon realize what is needed. Spying a pay phone on Václavské nám., the international operator is soon instructed to place a collect call and state that it is 'an emergency'. Sia, whose kind soul always keeps her phone on for the duration of the night in case her friends need her, answers.

'Wanna go to The Model?

'Wait...' Laughter. We breathe a sigh of relief. 'You guys are back? The operator said this was an emergency?'

'It is. We're extremely sad.'

It does our hearts much good to talk to them as the phone is passed to Jess and Kelly also. Jess awesomely volunteering to pay for the conversation, which, depending on whose memory you trust, comes to anywhere between $50-200. In the end, months later, Sia convinces an amiable AT&T employee to waive the charges. Bolstered in spirit, Andy letting out a few more Praha howls along the way, the clock is approaching 3 AM as we stumble back to our fourth hostel in four days.

VII – 'An Answer That Refused To Be Found'

With our flight leaving Tempelhof the next afternoon, it is time for us to head back to Germany. I recall nothing between getting out of bed and arriving at Hlavni Nadrazi station for the 12:07 PM train to Berlin Zoologischer Garten, as if Memory unleashed a veil to descend and protect our lonesome hearts. A deep sadness lurking in those hours, unwise to revisit. For we have to face the fact that we are never going to see Hanna and Eirin again. We continue to hope of course, as we make our way through streets lively with a football match in the air, that their longed-for faces might appear somewhere amidst the throng. But as we take our seats on the train, we are forced to acknowledge the truth. As Andy put it, he'd been 'defeated by his own vanity'.

Settling into the carriage, Andy cracks open a beer, I Nabokov's *The Eye*. As the departure whistle blows, two twenty-something females open our compartment door. Could they join us? Of course. Though I'm not so sure. There is an implicit quiet between Andy and I that need not be broken. We could spend the journey regrouping - drinking, in a book, ruminating in solitude - arriving in Berlin all the better for it. Conversation with these two schoolteachers would greatly get in the way of me getting some reading done.

Talk is buoyant, however. For the first few minutes at least. But once we explain our predicament, these women don't understand anything about it at all – why we had come to Europe in the first place, how we could not have spoken to the girls immediately when we saw them again in Prague, and why we would ever spend our time being sad when there is so much partying to be done. Our highly romantic natures are as foreign to them as the Czech railway signs all around us.

Some ways down the line, in an effort to salvage the situation, one of the women pulls out a bowl, informing us they'd chosen our compartment because we 'looked like we'd be cool with weed'. Andy indulges. I scowl, explaining that smoking will interfere with my reading. They laugh, 'you've been on the same page for an hour now'. Which, I have to admit, is true. But I would have been much further along had I just been left alone in accordance with my wishes. I have always been highly sensitive to marijuana, and even with such smoke in the air now, I could not concentrate as fully on *The Eye* as I would have liked, as fully as I had brought it to Europe for. The atmosphere in the carriage returns to its initial silence, with an even more uncomfortable timbre. These women are not happy about having us as travelling companions. They chastise themselves for choosing the wrong seats and make no bones about expressing their disappointment as any chance of an enjoyable journey disappears back behind the Czech border, beyond the horizon.

The four of us do not say goodbye. Total silence reigns as we head in purposely opposite directions when the train finally pulls into the station. Andy and I set out for Backpackers, the other hostel besides Circus that we've been hearing is a blast. Somehow becoming efficient travelers in the midst of all this, we had phoned ahead to book two beds for this our last night in Berlin. A city we've perhaps spent all of twenty hours awake and not hallucinating in since we arrived seven days ago to find Nick Cave's bar.

Upon approaching Backpackers' front desk, we learn that there has been yet another mix-up and we are once again shuffled off to another non-descript room in a forgotten establishment down the road. Still needing some time away from each other, I set out to find a postcard for Terri back in the States. I miss her. The black and white card I eventually choose featuring a long grey dismal-yet-grand Berlin boulevard stretching off into the distance. Empty, completely empty. It sums up Andy and my experience to a T.

Returning to our new room, resolving to make the most of things, and finding Andy has done the same. We hatch a plan to take a quick nap and then head out into the night, finally taking advantage of what this great city has to offer. We lay down at 8 PM, ready to rise in a few hours.

After a solid twelve hours sleep, we awake the next morning at 8 AM, any feeling of refreshment from such a slumber greatly eclipsed by the knowledge that we have wasted our last night in Germany. The sense of loss is palpable. Being guys who don't really know what to do when confronted with Morning, at least not without a run-up of drunken witching hours to it, we are in no further hurry to get out of bed. The one regret I've had in the years since - the one we could have tangibly done something about - is why didn't we at least try to go see Hansa Studios? Where The Birthday Party had recorded the *Mutiny!* and *Bad Seed* eps, and Cave had done *The Firstborn Is Dead*, *Your Funeral...My Trial*, and, yes, mixed that fateful *Kicking Against The Pricks*. A simple visit would have gone a long way towards redemption and, who knows, could have given us a whole different perspective on our trip. I'd have loved to have seen that studio. I still would. But for me to be able to truthfully tell you we went there would make too much sense.

Our flight to Luxembourg, where we are due to spend the evening laidover as a condition of our return fare, is departing at 4 PM. We leave our lodgings around 11, making our way to the general vicinity of Tempelhof Airport. Hansa Studios isn't even a consideration at this point, it's not until years later that the thought even occurs to me. So what can we do to make the most of our final hours?

After a languorous walk, stupefied by all that hadn't happened, with 45 minutes left until check-in time, we spot our shot at redemption - five döner kebab stands positioned between us and the airport doors. Andy deciding to down a beer at every one of them. A noble pursuit, to recoup what we could of our squandered time. The procession echoing that of the trip thus far. As we countdown five, four, three it's all bright and optimistic – big smiles, big beers. Then a deep weariness setting in at Victoria Grill for the penultimate beverage. At the final stop, mission accomplished, Andy slamming his emptied can down on the tabletop, quickly followed by his own head, arms raised with the last coin to his name in one hand and Hanna's handwritten note in the other. A gesture, and curious mixture, of victory in defeat.

We arrive in Luxembourg by 6 PM on one of those long European summer evenings that seem to stretch out forever. Checking into our hotel, again courtesy of my mother and the travel agent, again not very near anything at all. It is the last night of the trip *totale* and although not in Berlin anymore, we are determined to have a good time.

Which, for me, involves soup. I had gotten a taste for *crème de tomates* whilst traveling with Terri the previous autumn and now, once again finding myself in a French-speaking country, I reckon I would be insane not to take advantage of my proximity to the desired dish. Despite it being a summer Thursday, nothing seems to be open except for one fancy restaurant that we eventually circle back to, seating ourselves outside in the cool evening breeze. The waitress is not happy with me only ordering a bowl of soup and doing so in a mixture of such badly-accented-grammared-and-pronounced broken French and English. Andy stepping in to ask for a peace-making bottle of red. We are down to the last of the cash and I'm nervous lest my credit card not be accepted when we might need it, and even so, I'm not prepared to go into any more debt, even for this most delicious soup. Over our rouged dinner I recall how amused Andy would be when, back in Allston, he'd hear France Gall intone 'pantalones' while 'Nous Ne Sommes Pas Des Anges' blared on my car stereo. I set about teaching him some basic French phrases. A language I've always wanted to be able to speak better myself. The trouble being that my college classes began at 8 AM, and arriving drunk having been up all night were not the ideal conditions for learning. But I knew enough to describe my French as 'piss-pauvre'.

Finishing up, we purchase some cans of beer and head into the valley in the midst of the city, the one I'd been so enchanted by during my brief stop-off with Terri the year before. Sitting on the stone walls suspended across this gorge, we down Carlsbergs and local brews, discussing Love. Andy soon vomiting over the edge, not so much a commentary on our chosen topic as a pronouncement upon our journey, now almost at its end.

With cans and guts emptied, we head back to the city center, shocked to find almost everything shut at only ten at night. Circling and circling the few main streets until we hear the boisterous sounds of a bar. Upon entering, it seems as if everyone is having a grand old time and there are plenty of girls about. It looks like just the place for us. The bouncer asks Andy to remove his ever-present Misfits baseball cap. Andy misunderstanding and refusing, resulting in us being denied entry. Back to the drawing 'bourg.

Out walking the same path again, over and over, as if our recirculant steps were tracing the magical symbols necessary to conjure a drinking establishment from thin air. After enough time has passed for our unconscious spell to take shape, we notice a recessed doorway with a light on. Not too bright, not wishing to call attention to itself. No windows, the building itself painted all black. But still, a beacon of hope.

Finding the door locked, we look at each other, take a deep breath, and knock. Which is unusual to do at a bar.

And then even more strange, a slat slides open at eye level. 'Oui?' comes a female voice. 'We'd like to drink.' The panel slamming back, but to our great relief we hear what seems to be a series of locks being undone. Most unusual for a bar. This procedure is puzzling, though not as perplexing as the fact that a beer costs ten dollars, and even more so that the room is empty except for a couple in a dark corner and a large screen in the center of the room showing a pornographic film. Not wishing to bother the only other two patrons, we seat ourselves on the couch directly in front of the screen, feeling very awkward indeed. All we want is to keep drinking. Sipping in tense silence, we soon realize that it is not so much a couple in the corner as a business transaction. As soon as our glasses are emptied we get the hell out of there.

"You know that bouncer from the last place just wanted you to take your hat off so we could go in?"

'Oh? I can do that.'

Said bouncer is none too pleased to see our faces again. Standing there with cap in hand though, the dark clouds over our heads begrimed with accumulated hardship and despair, the doorman becomes momentarily sympathetic to our plight. Ushering us over to a booth, his compassionate look conveying that just what we need lays within these four walls. There's music and plenty of girls. Things are looking up.

Soon two very attractive young ladies come and sit with us and we can't believe our luck. They're very friendly. And very touchy-feely. Andy and I grinning at each other. All this attention after such a rough nine days. But as a stripper takes the stage that we hadn't noticed before, it becomes apparent that these two very friendly young women mean something more when they ask us to buy them drinks. Forcing us to come clean and utter that phrase that every prostitute must love to hear - 'We don't have any money.' They're up lickety-split, scowling and stomping off in the direction of the door. You've never seen sweetness turn to disgust in such record time. Within a minute our once-benevolent bouncer is ejecting us from the premises, looking genuinely disappointed in us as human beings.

Out on the streets again, a soft witching hour rain has descended. I buy a sausage bun with ketchup to soak up the sorrow while Andy sits down on the wet pavement, removes his hat for a second time that night, and, holding it out to passersby, mutters his newly acquired French phrase, 'S'il vous plait'. No money finds its way into said *chapeau* and we soon give up this enterprise, catching an all-too-expensive cab back up the hills to our hotel.

The trip blacks out for me here. I remember nothing of the return flight and very little of the drive home from New Jersey to Boston. We listen to mix tapes and talk our usual talk, stopping in Darien for Duchess, The Nutmeg State's superior fast food chain. Passing road signs for Berlin, Connecticut off of I-91, I conjecture 'maybe we should have just gone there'.

Arriving back in Allston after nightfall, we make our way up the dilapidated steps to Andy's apartment intent on phoning much-missed friends and heading to The Model. But everyone is busy. We'll catch up tomorrow. After the phone is replaced on its receiver following the final call, we settle into the dark living room and press play on *Nick Cave & The Bad Seeds: The Videos.*

Post-Script One – 'This World Around', Zurich July 2009

'Have you ever woken up in Zurich, not quite sure how you've gotten there?' – a text from me to Sean Drinkwater of Boston synth-pop heroes Freezepop, July 24th, 2009

I was exaggerating for effect, but he didn't know that, nor did I let on. But my Livejournal entry for the day clearly states:

in order to combat this evergrowing sense of malaise (and hopefully not 'becoming more like Slothrop'), I'm fucking off to Switzerland for a bit.

2009 was a dark time for almost everyone I know. 'The Oxford Dons' came out of it – Jamie Manners' and my surrealist comedy where I play Don Johnson, a blacklisted CIA agent come to England where he finds Donald Fox, the Professor of 18th Century Albanian Poetry at Christnose College. Together we solved crimes. This absurd idea, inspired by a comment our friend Pippa made at London's Black Plastic club one night in September, and hinted at in that Belgian frites shop with Terri all those years ago, kept us laughing, getting us through the rest of the year. But those pre-autumn days were especially rough. I was drinking too much, even for me, and pining over a crush, to quote Cave again, the ghost of which still lingered on, though any possible interest on her part was long gone.

I had been living in London on and off since 2003, and steadily now since 2007. Zurich seemed to keep calling me back as I would reminisce about its lovely environs, my visit to Joyce's grave after Terri and I parted ways back in 1998 still strong in my memory. I finally read *Ulysses* in 2007, followed quickly by Richard Ellman's excellent Joyce biography. The former inspiring many titles for me, including one of the best songs I ever wrote, 'Boulevards In Blume'. And now this late-July 2009, I made plans at the beginning of the week to fly out on Friday, excited to be staying at the James Bond-named hotel, Fleming's, from which I sent Mr. Drinkwater the above text.

True to Berlin form, the hotel is booked for the rest of the weekend and upon waking I have to locate further lodging for the next two nights. Nowhere is affordable, nothing in Switzerland really is, though they do have the most attractively coloured money. I spend the day wandering the city, revisiting Fluntern Cemetery complete with a stop at Katalog Record Warehouse en route uphill on the number 6 tram, eating a lot, reading my beloved J.P. Donleavy, and, as my journal states, *downing dark beers at an alarming rate.*

Solitary and pleasantly on my way to such a state of inebriation as I was, there is only one person in the world who would fully understand the situation. I begin texting Andy, who is at work in New York City. My journal picks this up:

Drunk & full, I wander up to Bellevue for a glorious gaze upon the lake. Wandering its populated-by-young-lovers-but-otherwise-lonely shores, feeling a lot like Balthazar B. Stopping to get some writing done, which I quite like. Continuing to text Andy on all matters of life, laughter, & heartache. Until soon receiving the text:

'I'm starting to have a hard time following you.'

Nonetheless, it feels great to be in touch with my old best friend. The joy in the ridiculous, and the acceptance of the sad, to make it even more of both. Just like we used to do. For in recent years, since simultaneously leaving Allston, Massachusetts in 2004, we haven't seen each other that much, living in different states then countries, keeping in touch dwindling as a result, as it so often does. But if there is one man who would appreciate the Donleavy-esque circumstances I now find myself in, I know it would be Andy.

With my communications turning towards the incomprehensible, retiring for the evening seems like a good idea. Taking another tram back towards my hotel however, my journal picks up a different story:

A rather stunning blonde catches my eye and smiles. I smile back and quietly take my seat. Noticing her look over a few more times, and seeing she is accompanied by another striking blonde and an ubercute brunette. & three dudes. Who happen to be speaking

English. The tram pulls into a stop I recognize and all seven of us

alight. Risking it (addressing the dudes), 'Excuse me, I couldn't

help hearing you guys speak English. Are there any places open now

to get a drink?' The first blonde, Lucy, pushes her way through to

me. 'Hello, who are you with? Ah, you're all alone. In that case I

invite you to come join us.' & we proceed to Paddy O'Reilly's, an

Irish chain bar. They are all supernice & fun. Ramona, the

striking blonde, and Judi the ubercute brunette. The dudes are Rene,

a loveable jovial Czech, Patrick, a very friendly Canadian, &

Mico.

It turns out Lucy is with Mico, and this very hip Israeli

entrepreneur is refreshingly superenthusiastic about everything.

'Man, this is Zurich! Just grab the next girl who walks by and

make out with her!' I point to the man walking past, 'but that's a

dude.' Mico: 'It doesn't matter! This is Zurich!'

By this point Ramona has already left and I am way into
Judi anyway. After the DJ plays the entire *Blues Brothers*
soundtrack straight through, we take a cab to Patrick's for
the afterparty. Patrick going to get supplies, returning
with an eight-pack of Feldschlossen cans - a good Swiss

beer, a bottle of whisky, a bottle of rum, and snacks. US & Swiss currency are about equal and this totals 140 CH Francs. Wow. Mico & Lucy throwing a 100 down on the table, me only having a 50 on me and trying to give them some cash. They won't hear of it. I had just bought a $60 round at the bar. These wonderful people have made me feel very welcome and I spend most of the party talking to Judi, appreciating the magic that sometimes brings nights like these to you.

Around 3.30 Judi needs to catch the last train as she lives 25 minutes outside of the city. I offer to walk her to the station. There's an exchange in German instigated by Lucy, with Judi assuring her that it will be fine. We cab it then walk. I mention I might be going to Basel the next day. Tired, she perks up, 'I think I'm going to Basel too. Yes, I am going to Basel tomorrow for a friend I don't really like's party.'

Me, shy as ever, 'If we're both going to be in Basel, can I give you a call?'

'Yes. Yes, of course.' And she promptly gives me her number and a peck on the cheek before jumping on her train, which was then departing.

And now of course how Fate plays into all this. By her own admission, Judi was very forgetful. Shortly after we got to the Irish bar she told me 'I can never remember anything. The names of bands or songs I like. Even authors' names or characters in books or the names of the books themselves. Same for films.' And as we were leaving the party I had to point out that her wallet was still sitting on the table right in front of her.

As I walk away from the station, all alight from my kiss on the cheek and the prospect of spending the next day with this beautiful woman in Basel, I remember something. And it starts to gnaw at me. I'd been having such a good time, it had quickly gone out of my mind as soon as it happened, and wasn't there at all when I asked for her number. But thinking back to when we had arrived at the afterparty, Judi had lost her phone, which she had had at the bar. Lucy calling it to no avail, and the bar long closed. Judi was concerned about this for a few minutes then seemed to forget all about it for the rest of the night. How was I ever going to get in touch with her?

But I feel too good about things to let this hiccup undo me. I seem to be lost again, at an unfamiliar station in an unrecognized part of town. This is all fine. I let the night take me where it will and soon come across sights I know. Though what is about to enter my field of vision is completely unprecedented, and if heralded at all, by what, I cannot perceive.

It is 4 AM and two young men and a female companion careen around the corner pulling a make-shift boat - wheelbarrow, long paint-roller mast, sheet for a sail – and they are making their way down the street straight towards me. They don't really speak English but the girl, quite pretty & seemingly nice, tells me what is up when I ask. 'These two gentlemen love each other madly and want to get married and live together but the government will not let them so they are out now to raise money to do so.' Fantastic, I thought. If anything ever deserved money it is this pre-dawn display, and in the name of Love to boot. I hand her a 10 franc note, which the woman says they couldn't possibly accept. But on my insistence, she gives me change and I toss 3 CH francs into the wheelbarrow. By this time a crowd has begun to gather, and a very drunk man stumbling by believes the paint-roller to be a television camera, with him stopping to look around in the hopes of being interviewed. I continue to converse with the trio and soon talk turns to London. She had just been staying in Peckham Rye, and has some pretty horrible things to say about it. I recoil in horror, 'have I just given money to racists?' But the men seem nice enough, they couldn't be. I embrace the two young hopefuls and wish them all the best as I depart for my hotel, which takes me another hour to find.

Finally hopping on a bus heading in the direction of my bed, I text Sean Drinkwater again. Freezepop are celebrating their 10th anniversary by playing two sets – daytime and evening – at Harper's Ferry, now Brighton

Music Hall, back in Allston, MA. I drunkenly calculate that with the time difference, they'll still be onstage and my request might just get through.

MeText: Play Swiss Genius Girl (a pun on their hit 'Science Genius Girl')
SeanText: Okay.
MeText: Dedicate it to the mother of my children?
SeanText: Already did.
MeText: Nice!...I don't know where I am...
SeanText: Again? Oh man. Politely ask.

Tickled pink by this, I step off the bus, and dial Andy to leave a long and rambling message, complete with a plethora of verbal 'high-fives'. If he thought I was unintelligible eight hours ago...

Regaining my room, I'm now on its balcony, clad only in my boxer shorts, watching the sunrise and thankful for this new morning with all its promises of meeting Judi in Basel. The magic sweeping over the previous hours continues as Andy soon phones me back. I don't mention my lack of clothes and we proceed to have, as my journal states, *one hell of an awesome conversation.* Talking about everything, catching up through the years, listening and laughing and it is wonderful. He tells me of his recent trip to Japan, to visit the young lady he had been seeing in New York. I inform him of my night out with the Swiss. Expressing my concerns that this call could cost him a fortune, he says he doesn't care. I'm also silently worried that I might be charged for being outside my UK service area. And I want to be sure I have money on my phone to ring Judi the next day, or rather later today. I soon become aware that my battery is almost dead too, and that I have left my charger back in my flat on Holloway Road, some six hundred miles away. But as we laugh, none of this matters. We're international again, and however any of it might turn out, all is well in this moment.

Post-Script Two – 'The Corner Of My Room', Stratford, Connecticut 2019

I write this now, twenty years hence, in my hometown of Stratford, CT. The very place we'd decided Andy would say he was from when we were concocting a completely unnecessary backstory as part of our attempt to obtain his birth certificate from Tewksbury Town Hall. In the two decades that have passed, my love for the tale of this trip has only grown stronger and stronger. I'd tell it in the face of many a listener's firm doubts that Nick Cave ever owned a bar in Berlin. Which seems almost immaterial at this point, and something I've decided I never really want to know for sure. Even if Mr. Cave himself denied it, I wouldn't fully believe him. For we've come to realize that 'Nick Cave's Bar' was the metaphysical state we were living in at the time. The true name of 'The Dark Carnival', of which that appellation was only an antechamber. How easy it was to step through the thin ethereal veil, separating our own mistakenly-believed-humdrum existence, into the wild world The Bad Seeds songs spoke of and that resonated so much with our truest dreams.

A lot has changed since then, as by rights it should have. Andy has run a successful art gallery in New York City for over a decade. I stopped drinking seven years ago. I got tired of the existential crises that after two days of agony I'd realize was only a hangover. I always said I'd take it up again for the duration of the trip if we ever went back to try and find the bar one more time, perhaps on the 20th anniversary of our initial quest. Those dates have now passed by a few weeks and I'm glad we didn't. It's not good to attempt to relive the past. And as over the course of his career, Mr. Cave's songs progressed from ones of dark poetry screaming themselves alive with often disturbing dissonance to beautifully romantic love songs steeped in a more mature heart, so have our own lives.

Spooked and nagged by it as I was at first sight, I keep coming back to finding *Kicking Against The Pricks*, the covers album, in Prague. Not our initial destination at all.

And in line with this idea of 'Nick Cave's Bar' being a metaphysical space, one we stepped into at will and which soon gained material substance, perhaps we were ourselves covering the concept there, in Europe. Something that had only existed ethereally, until we made it real. Our own version, where - like Cave singing The Pogues, on the flipside of his 'What A Wonderful World' duet with Shane MacGowan, one of our favourites from that much-watched video collection – we sang all our sorrows, to now tell you them in joy.

Post-Script Three – 'Death Is Not The End', 2020

On New Years Day 2016 I woke up in my apartment in Ashland, Massachusetts and drew three Tarot cards from Jodorowsky's original Marseille deck. One of which, the Four of Pentacles, bears a Phoenix in its center. I became quite taken with this image, intent as I was on leaving town, rising from Ashland like the famous mythical bird. I soon got the unshakeable sense that Phoenix, Arizona would be important to me. And, when at the end of that year, I decided to relocate to Los Angeles, I divert my course to be sure to stop in the Arizona capital along the way. Turning off US 40 towards my intermediate destination, I drive through the most beautiful scenery I have ever laid eyes on. Over snowy mountaintops with their majestic fir trees, soon descending out of this Narnia into lush green. Onwards over one-lane desert roads that GPS refuses to reach, until out of nowhere, Phoenix rises upon the horizon. I feel an immediate affection for the city, particularly its vegan restaurants Nami and Green, and will make sure to stop here on any future cross-country treks.

Come February 2020 and after a long year back in Connecticut, I'm ready to return to California a.s.a.p. I have a temp job lined up and the plan is to perform comedy at every opportunity, as much as I possibly can. Despite his increasingly hermit-like disposition, Andy and I have been in touch a lot more this past year. The three occasions he leaves the house during 2019 each being to one of my comedy shows. Come February for him, it's a trip to northern Arizona to see the sights. We realize this will coincide with my cross-country drive and I arrange to meet him. My goal on this particular coast-to-coast, besides restarting life again in LA, is to stand in the exact center of the continental United States, two miles north of Lebanon, Kansas, an idea I've grown increasingly fond of over the years. I make it to this mecca and linger over the very spot listening to Elvis, Van Halen, and Guided By Voices. And now it's high time to hightail it to AZ where Andy and I are due to meet.

The trip is oppressive. A late start alters my original plan of only spending eight hours a day in the car for the sake of my spine, to now having to cover 500 miles per solar cycle, a tight timetable further complicated by the busted headlight a police warning mandates I replace. Our initial plan to convene in Sedona, AZ on February 5th where Andy is renting a house is pushed to a hotel in Jerome on the 10th and finally to Phoenix the following day. Phoenix again. Though with my back now aching and the accumulated frustrations of solo car travel abounding, I doublecheck with Andy that I'm not impinging on his vacation. Much as I'd like to see him, if it turns out that getting together is a hassle, I can rest and take my time getting to LA.

'I would love to hang out' comes his response.

I buckle up and blast through the flatlands of Kansas, Oklahoma, and Texas. Stopping for a much needed breather in New Mexico. Really loving Albuquerque and wishing to spend more time there but for the need to press on. Arriving at my Studio 6 room in Tempe, AZ around 8PM, two hours later than planned. My road journal stating: *Joints all jelly, brain all mush. I'd told Andy I'd pick him up at his hotel and then we'd go to Green. But for the last* hour of my drive - 380 miles today - I knew I could not drive a second longer. I quickly check in, bring my stuff to my room while ordering a Lyft, texting Andy the plan and that I'll meet him there if he is up for it. Not much parking at the restaurant and I watch Andy swing around and park alongside a row of very tall bushes upon which the driver's side door would open. In my exhausted blurry state it seems like Andy might open the door into the bushes, step out, and disappear. Instead he chooses the passenger side door and we have quite a nice catch-up and meal. Myself having my first po boy - so delish I order a second - and bbq 'wings'.

Meeting up with Andy was my second objective on this trip, after standing in the center of the States, kept quiet in case any sideswipings sent me off course. I've half-heartedly been trying to convince him to go to the Warriors/Suns game tomorrow, as the first time I drove to Phoenix I got it in my head that going to a basketball game might be the thing to do. Tickets up top are going for a mere $7 a piece. We'll see how tomorrow goes. Maybe one day this will form a coda to my Nick Cave's Bar story show.

These last words give me chills when I read them now.

I pick Andy up around 3 PM the next day as he has decided to stay in bed while I explore the city's record shops. I saved the bookstores until he is in the car and off we go to Book Gallery, a large establishment whose fine wares impress us both. Opening tip off comes and goes as we sit in The Handlebar in Tempe, with Andy of course having no interest in attending a basketball game. Instead we head to the Phoenix Art Museum to experience one of Yayoi Kusama's Infinity Rooms. I know nothing about the artist or the wonderful spaces she's created, but visiting such here is one of Andy's goals for the trip, the lines to get in to her exhibits in New York being prohibitively long. I am enthralled and disoriented, in a very pleasing way.

After that, more vegan food at Earth Plant Based where I am delighted to learn that the gluten-free version of their 'Crazy Shrimp' is called 'Crazier Shrimp'. Then on to Cobra Arcade Bar where a bouncer asks to see our IDs. Two men about to turn forty-four, a testament to our youthful demeanors. We start with *Galaga* before moving on to two-player *1943*, *Tetris*, and pinball, the Iron Maiden machine particularly appealing.

The tokens having been spent, it was time to call it a night. I drop Andy off in front of his hotel, The Clarendon. It was the last time I ever saw him.

The preceding Post Script, number two, was supposed to be the final one for this book. I've never thought of myself as a P.P.P.S. kind of guy, but here we have it.

My dream of performing the *Nick Cave's Bar* story had come true. I put on the first show at Pete's Candy Store in Brooklyn on Saturday October 5th, 2019. Andy came and it felt fantastic to finally tell the tale live and to have him be there for it. Andy texted our friend Rick, 'It was really, really good. There was a good-sized crowd and people were laughing non-stop during the Nick Cave story. He killed it. I was really impressed and proud of him.' This meant the world to me, that my best friend, who I had shared the experience with and who had given me such encouragement about my writing over the years, approved. I took the show to Boston for a night at ONCE in Somerville on November 11th. As I began preparing to move to LA, the plan was to pick up the show there, and wherever else would have me, ideally around the world.

When COVID-19 hit, my Young Southpaw shows in the UK were cancelled, and who knows when we'll be performing again. By chance, my friend Tom had recorded the Brooklyn show of *Nick Cave's Bar* on his phone, and this book had already been finished the previous summer. In the spring of 2020, I decided that it would be best to release these and move on to other stories. Andy approving of this plan and thinking highly of both the show and the book. I began to get them ready for an autumn release.

And then on August 26th, the unthinkable happened. I got the phone call that Andy had passed away earlier that day. Eerily around the same time I was recording a trial run of the Zurich Post Script. Things forever changed. A part of me missing. He was like my brother and we went through so much together. It became important to get this story out, as planned, but now as even more of a tribute to our friendship. It meant so much to me in the days following his death just how many people got in touch to say they knew how close Andy and I were. One of my favourite comments being from my friend Craig, 'You could always tell how much admiration you guys had for each other. Even through the craziness of the NCB saga, which certainly would have been the undoing of lesser friendships.'

Of course too, Nick Cave covers 'By The Time I Get To Phoenix' on the *Kicking Against The Pricks* album, the record I made so much of on our Berlin trip.

Like I said, Andy and I had been in touch a lot this past year. I downloaded 262 pages of text messages between us from the time I got my new phone in October 2018 until August 2020. They contain so much of his genius sense of humor.

Now for a moment let me take you back to September 2007, the day after our friends Jen & Tony's wedding, and yet another long car ride I would be sharing with Andy, and his then-girlfriend Christine. We were caught in traffic and what should have taken a mere two-and-a-half hours was now extending upwards of four. Passing the time engaged in one of my favourite discussions, that of the most ridiculous band names that could possibly exist. Andy soon suggesting 'Portugal' and bursting out laughing. It was the first time I clocked the special significance that word had for him. Something about its sound really seemed to please him. Even funnier when we later found out about the band Portugal The Man, and the country name kept coming up after that, with increasing frequency.

Out of the blue one spring evening in 2019, Andy left me a voicemail beginning 'I mean who's to say the Portuguese didn't invent cinnamon rolls?', going on for thirty more seconds in the best Young Southpaw homage I've ever heard. On April 8th of this year, 2020, I was very surprised to get a text which simply read 'I wonder why Franco never invaded Portugal. I mean...c'mon'.

When on August 5th I asked Andy about his love of the word, he replied 'I feel like the Portuguese are 'hiding things' in general. Ever since I brought up the fact that they've never been conquered by Spain and completely stayed out of WWII. Although, I've learned a little bit about the former issue recently.' He then went on to tell me of their spice trading disputes. This blew both our minds as we soon recalled the subject matter of his Southpaw impersonation. As Andy put it, 'Turns out for like half a century they actually did have a monopoly on the cinnamon trade in Europe.'

Then on August 21st, shortly after midnight:

You're not going to believe this, but tonight I was watching Jeopardy with my roommate, which we try to do whenever possible. The Final Jeopardy category was European Borders. And apparently the oldest and most stable border in all of Europe since around 1220 is that between Spain and Portugal and I'd answered correctly. So I then bored her to death for 10 minutes explaining how 'Aug and I have been talking a lot about this recently.'

Followed 15 minutes later with:

I guess what I'm saying is that we may need to travel to the Portugal/Spain border to find Nick Cave's Bar. Because honestly, I'm tired of him being one step ahead of us.

I mean, when he was done with the UK and Berlin, where'd he go? São Paulo, the capital city in Brazil, the only country in the new world that speaks Portuguese as a national language.

Going on to point out that Nick Cave's song 'Foi Na Cruz' on *The Good Son* was based on a Brazilian hymn also used in the 1980 film, *Pixote*, starring Fernando Ramos da Silva. With the previous Nick Cave & The Bad Seeds album, *Tender Prey*, being dedicated to da Silva aka 'Pixote'.

I mean Pixote vs. Quixote? When Cave sings that 'it was on the cross.' He's clearly talking about crossing the Spanish/Portuguese border. It couldn't be any more clear where that bar is.

I'll meet you there, Andy.

2

Lightning Source UK Ltd.
Milton Keynes UK
UKHW011429240621
386089UK00002B/580

9 781087 929071